The DADGAD Gospel

Gospel Guitar Solos in DADGAD Tuning

El McMeen & Sandy Shalk

To access the online audio go to:
WWW.MELBAY.COM/30862MEB

The Brazilian Rosewood OM with Curly Redwood Top is courtesy of Franklin Guitar Company.
Photo by Notley Hawkins.

© 2021 Ellsworth McMeen and Sandy Shalk.
All rights reserved. Used by permission.
Exclusive Sales Agent: Mel Bay Publications, Inc.
WWW.MELBAY.COM

Contents

Title	Page	Audio
Preface	3	
The Music		
Blessed Assurance	4	1
Down in the River to Pray	8	2
Drifting Too Far from the Shore	12	3
Holy Manna	14	4
In Christ There is No East or West	16	5
In the Great Triumphant Morning	18	6
Just As I Am	20	7
Must Jesus Bear the Cross Alone	22	8
On Jordan's Stormy Banks	24	9
Softly and Tenderly	28	10
The Hallelujah Side	32	11
There Is Power in the Blood	34	12
What a Friend We Have in Jesus	36	13
When I Can Read My Title Clear	38	14
Whiter Than Snow	40	15
Will the Circle Be Unbroken	42	16
Yes, I Know	44	17

Preface

The great guitar tuning DADGAD, invented by the late British guitarist David ("Davey") Graham in the mid-20th Century, has provided the canvas for a variety of musical renderings in different genres. Mr. Graham himself played originals, Celtic music, jazz, middle-Eastern music, and other types of music in the tuning. It has been a mainstay of fingerstyle players around the world who have been exploring its endless possibilities.

Sandy Shalk, one of the authors of this book, has presented two lengthy DVD lessons of jazz and traditional music in DADGAD for Stefan Grossman's Guitar Workshop and Mel Bay Publications. Those lessons are entitled "Fingerstyle Guitar in DADGAD" and "Further Adventures in DADGAD." El McMeen has arranged many different types of music in various tunings, and has recorded DVD's for Stefan Grossman's Guitar Workshop and written books for Mel Bay Publications.

This folio focuses on the authors' arrangements of gospel music in DADGAD. It features some wonderful music that may be "below the radar" for fingerstyle guitar players but is well-known among gospel singing groups and their audiences. The level is generally for advanced beginner/intermediate players. That having been said, players may encounter some challenges in certain tunes if not familiar with the alternating-bass/"thumb-style" picking. Moreover, some of the arrangements have rich chordal support for the melody, and a player looking to simplify need only leave out some of the middle voices in the chords. Just be sure not to lose the melody in that approach.

We hope you enjoy playing this music as much as we enjoyed arranging it. Feel free to listen to sung versions of the tunes on the Internet to hear the phrasing and rhythms. That's what we did!

Best regards,

El and Sandy
NJ and Delaware

Blessed Assurance

Phoebe Palmer Knapp
Arr. Sandy Shalk

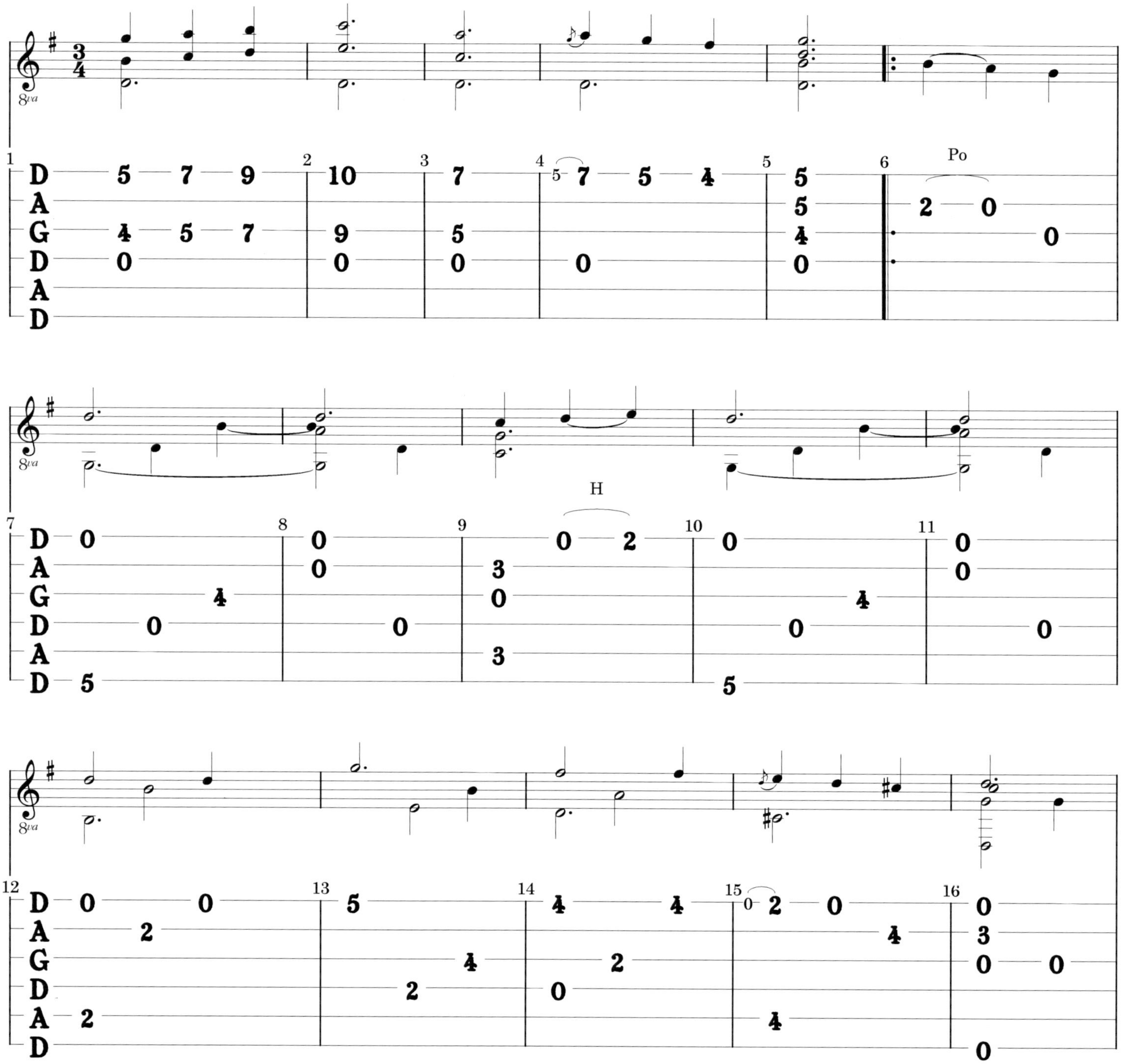

Blessed Assurance (Page 2/3)

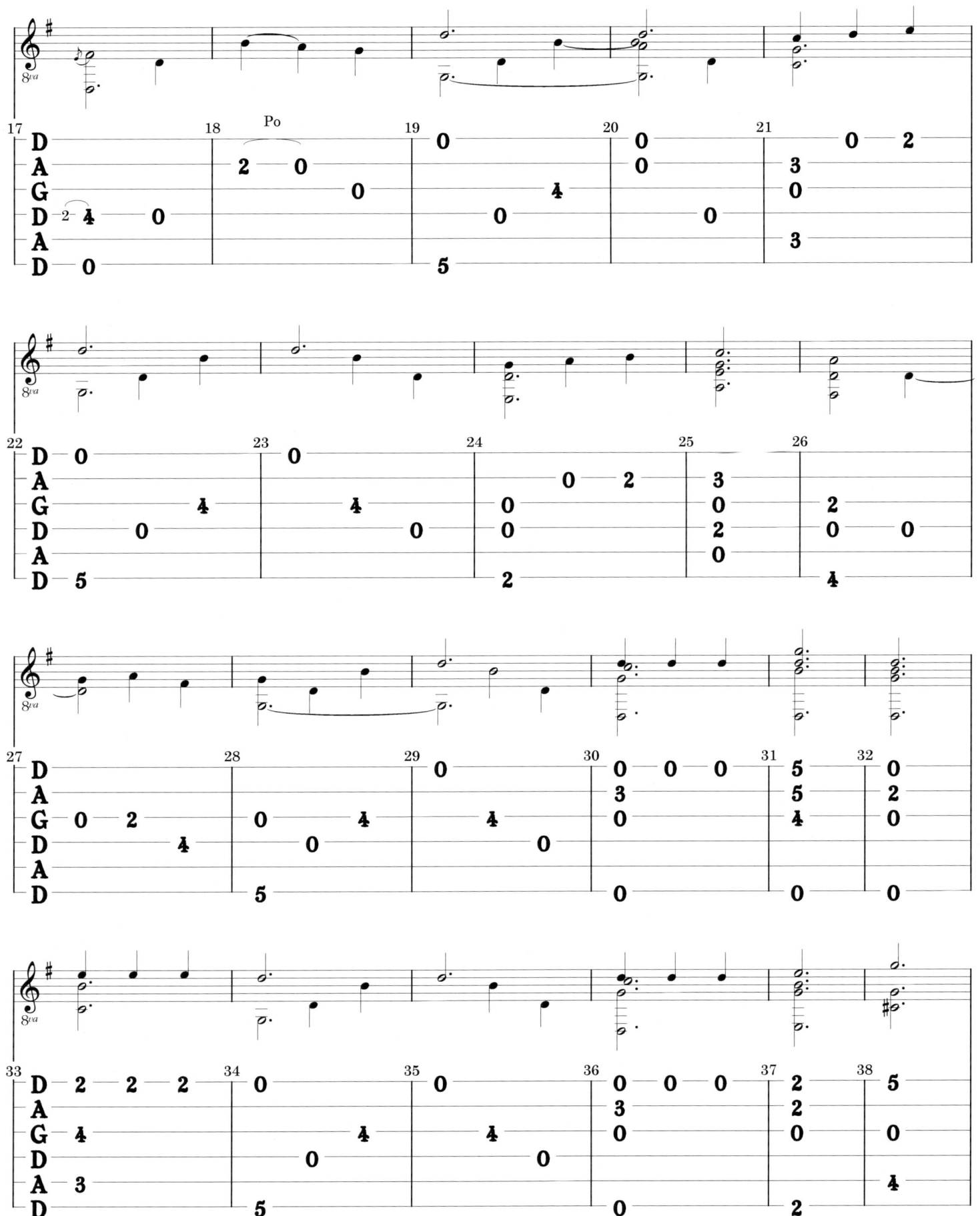

Blessed Assurance (Page 3/3)

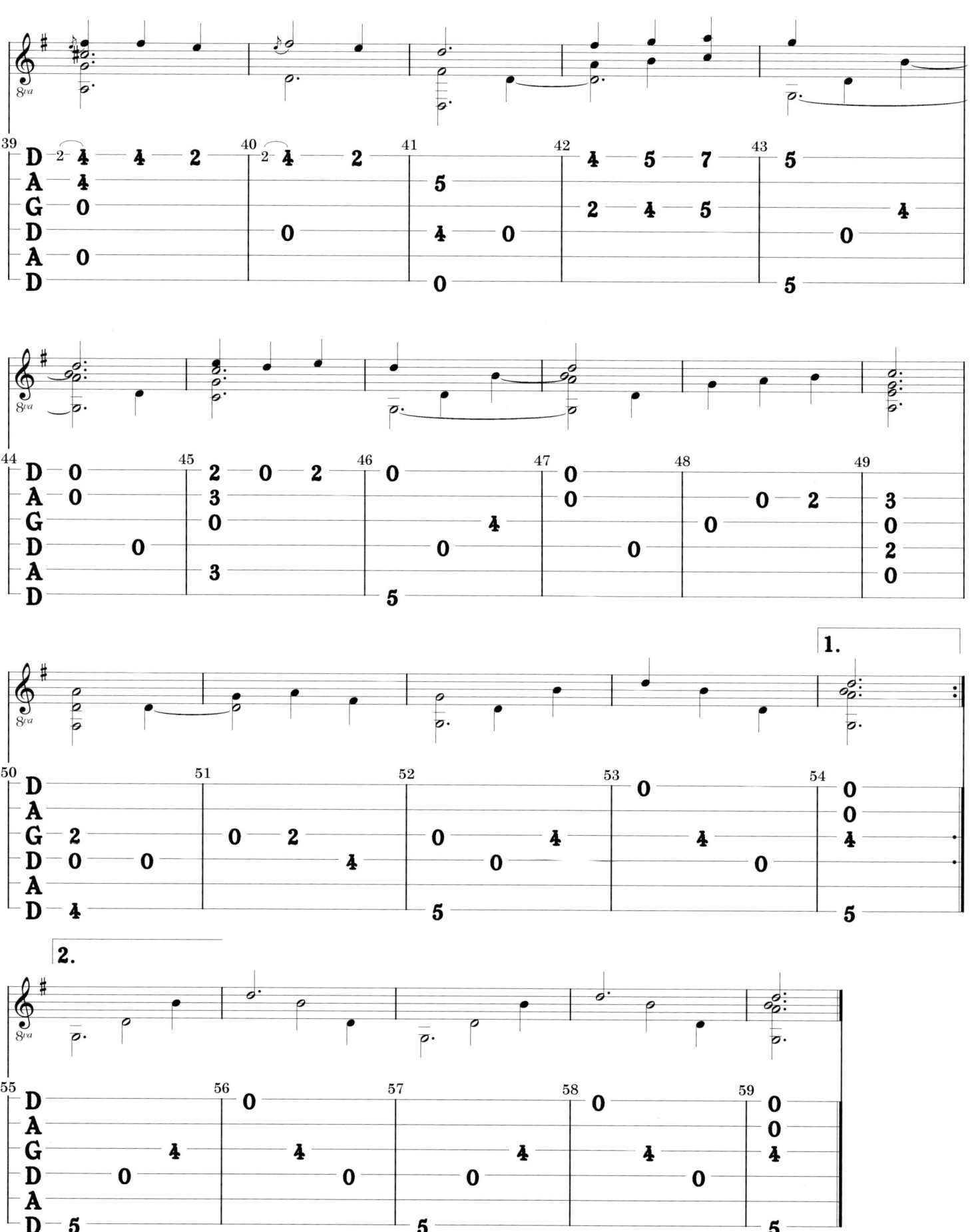

This page has been left blank to avoid an awkward page turn.

Down in the River to Pray

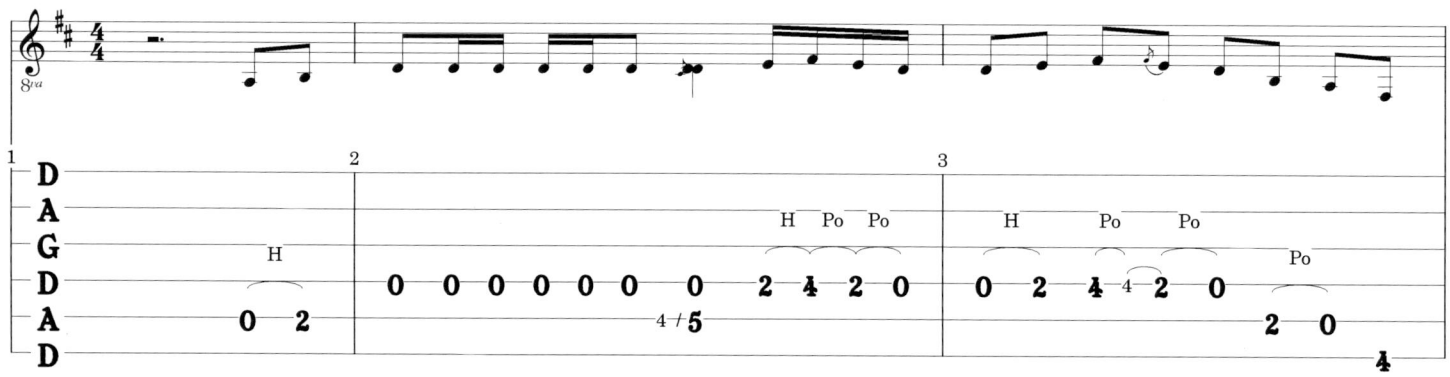
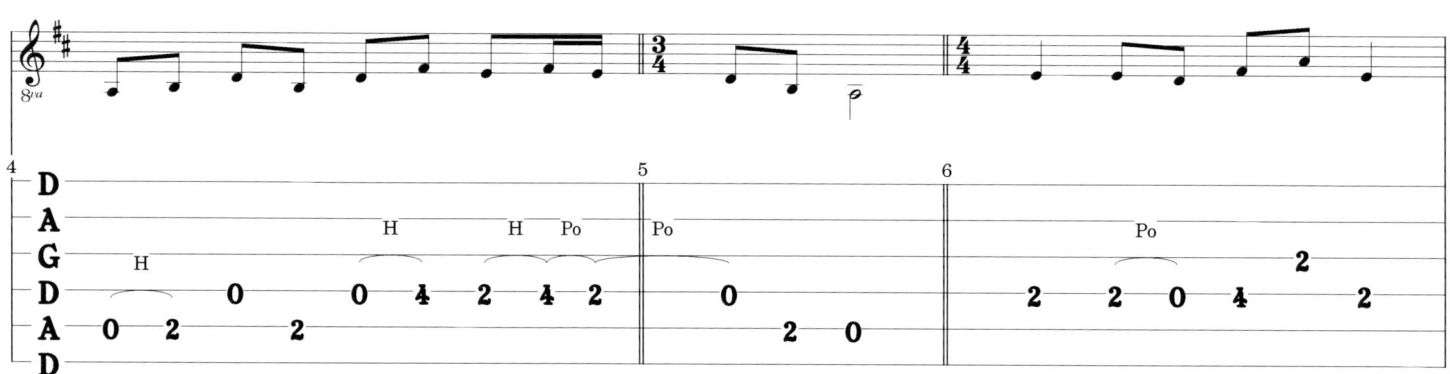
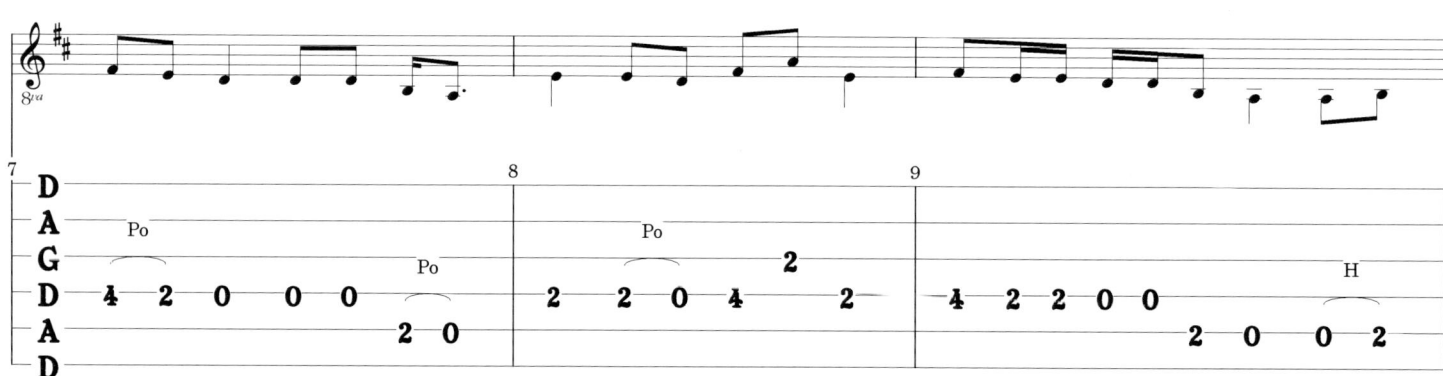
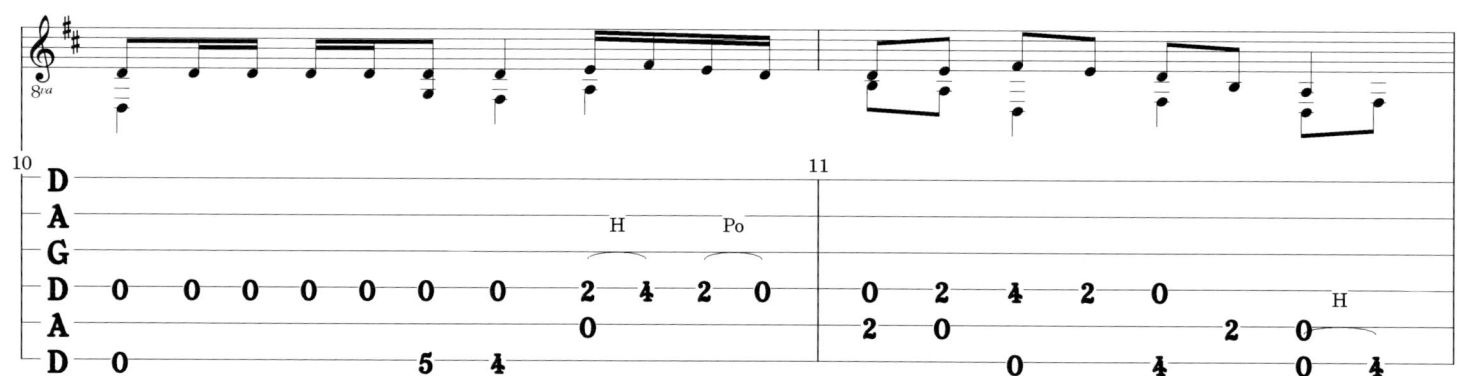

Guitar Arr. (c) 2019 Ellsworth McMeen. All Rights Reserved. Used by Permission.

Down in the River to Pray (Page 2/3)

Down in the River to Pray (Page 3/3)

This page has been left blank to avoid an awkward page turn.

Drifting Too Far from the Shore

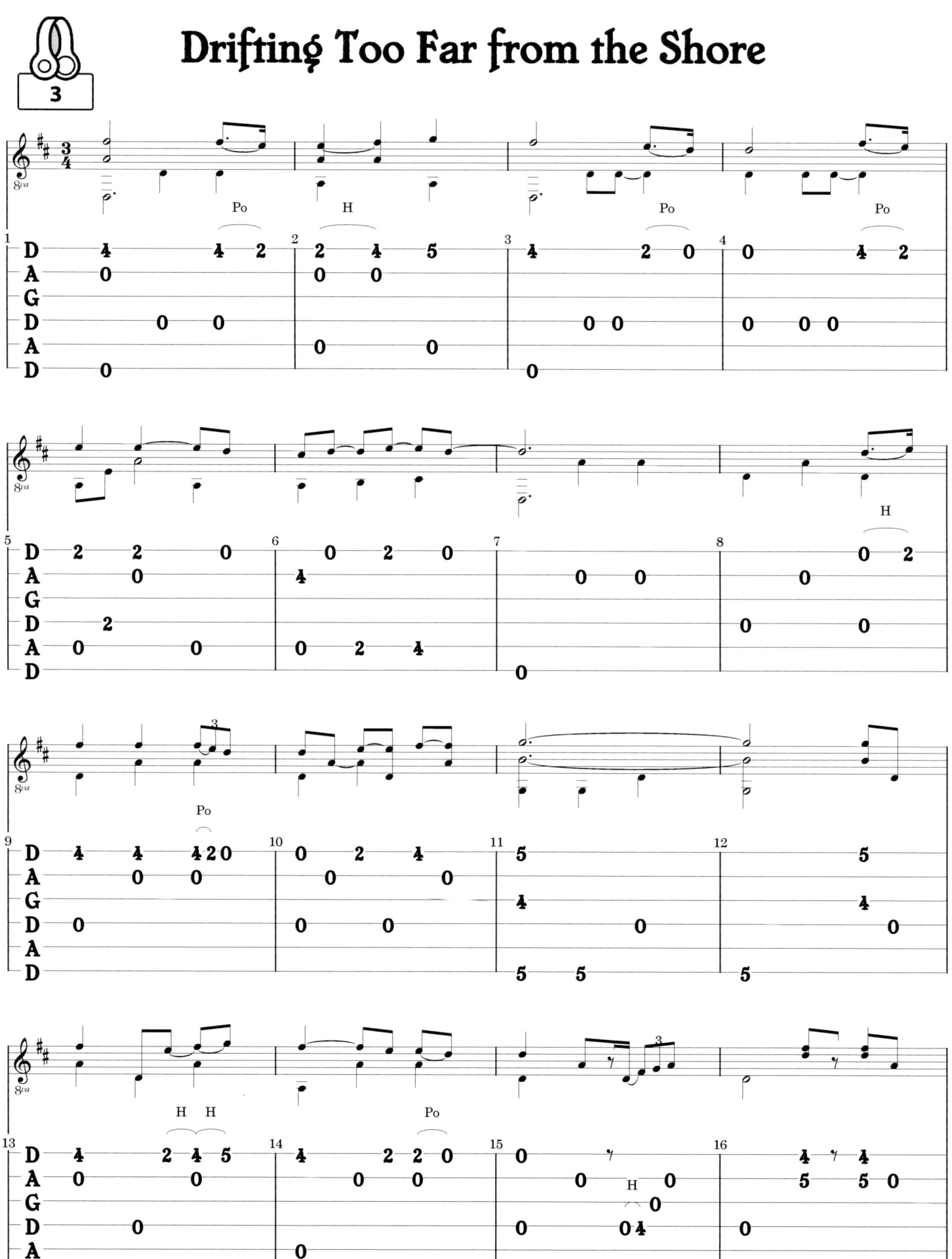

Guitar Arr. (c) 2019 Ellsworth McMeen. All Rights Reserved. Used by Permission.

Drifting Too Far from the Shore (Page 2/2)

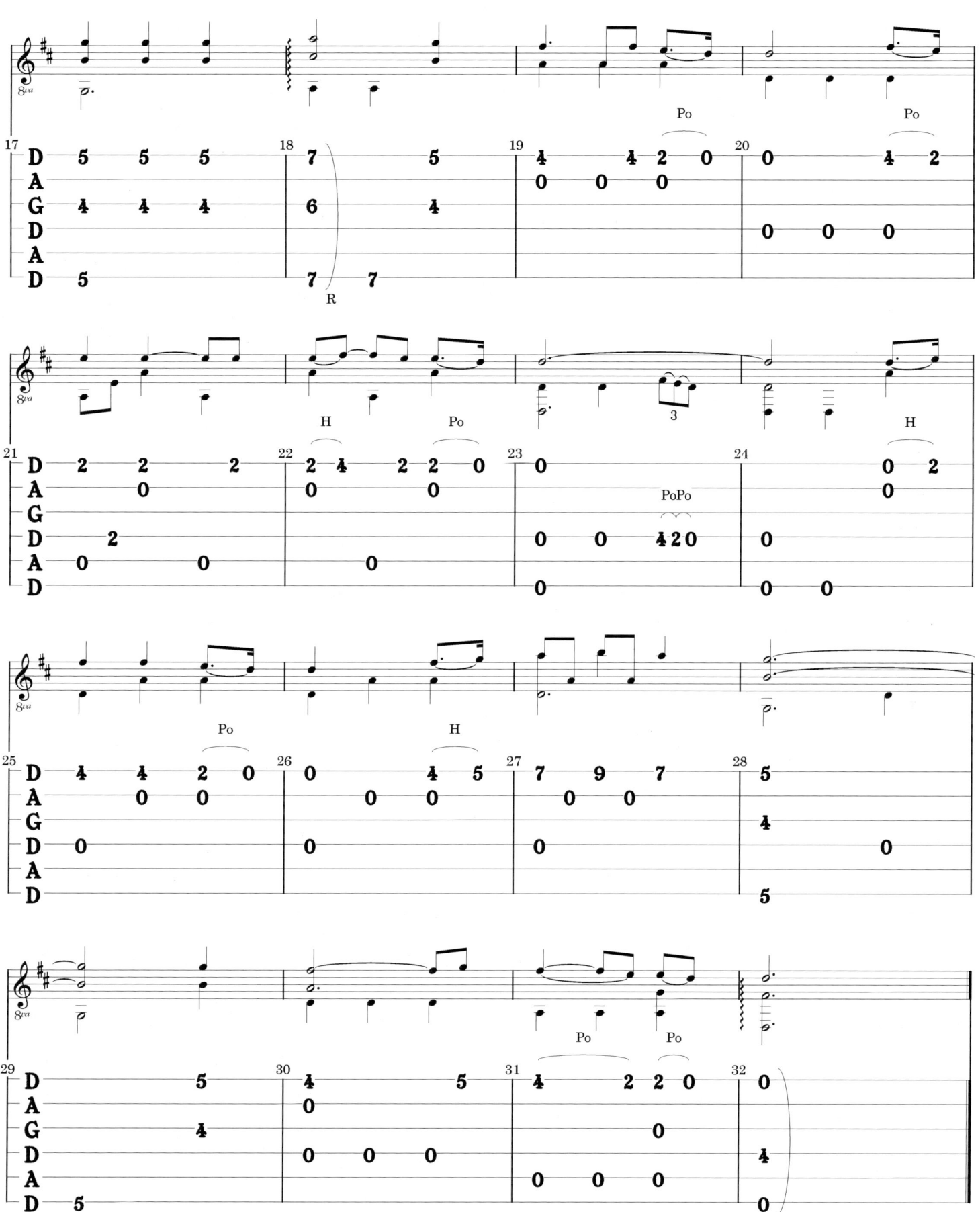

Holy Manna

Wm. B. Bradbury
Arr. Ellsworth McMeen

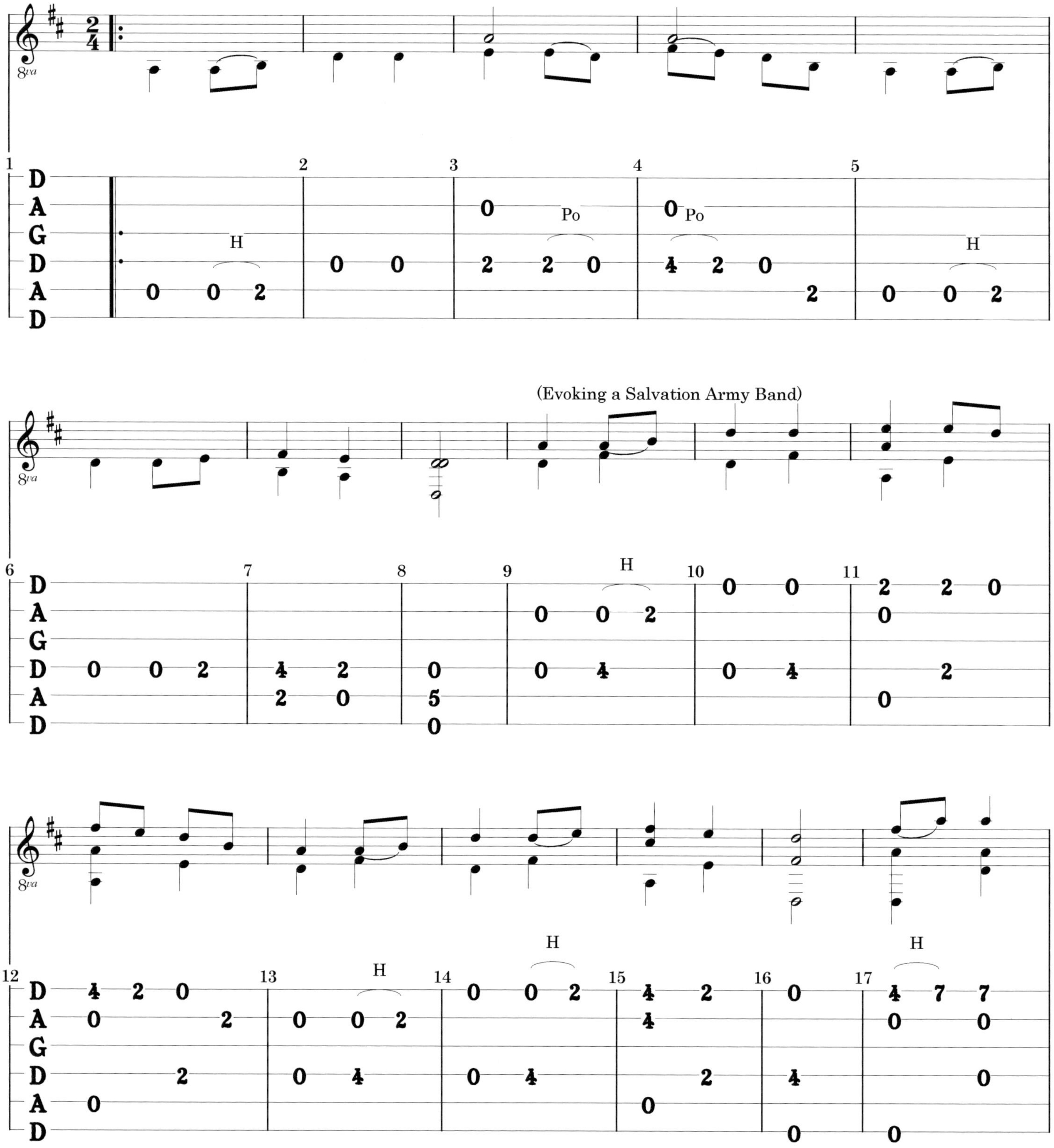

Guitar Arr. (c) 2019 Ellsworth McMeen. All Rights Reserved. Used by Permission.

Holy Manna (Page 2/2)

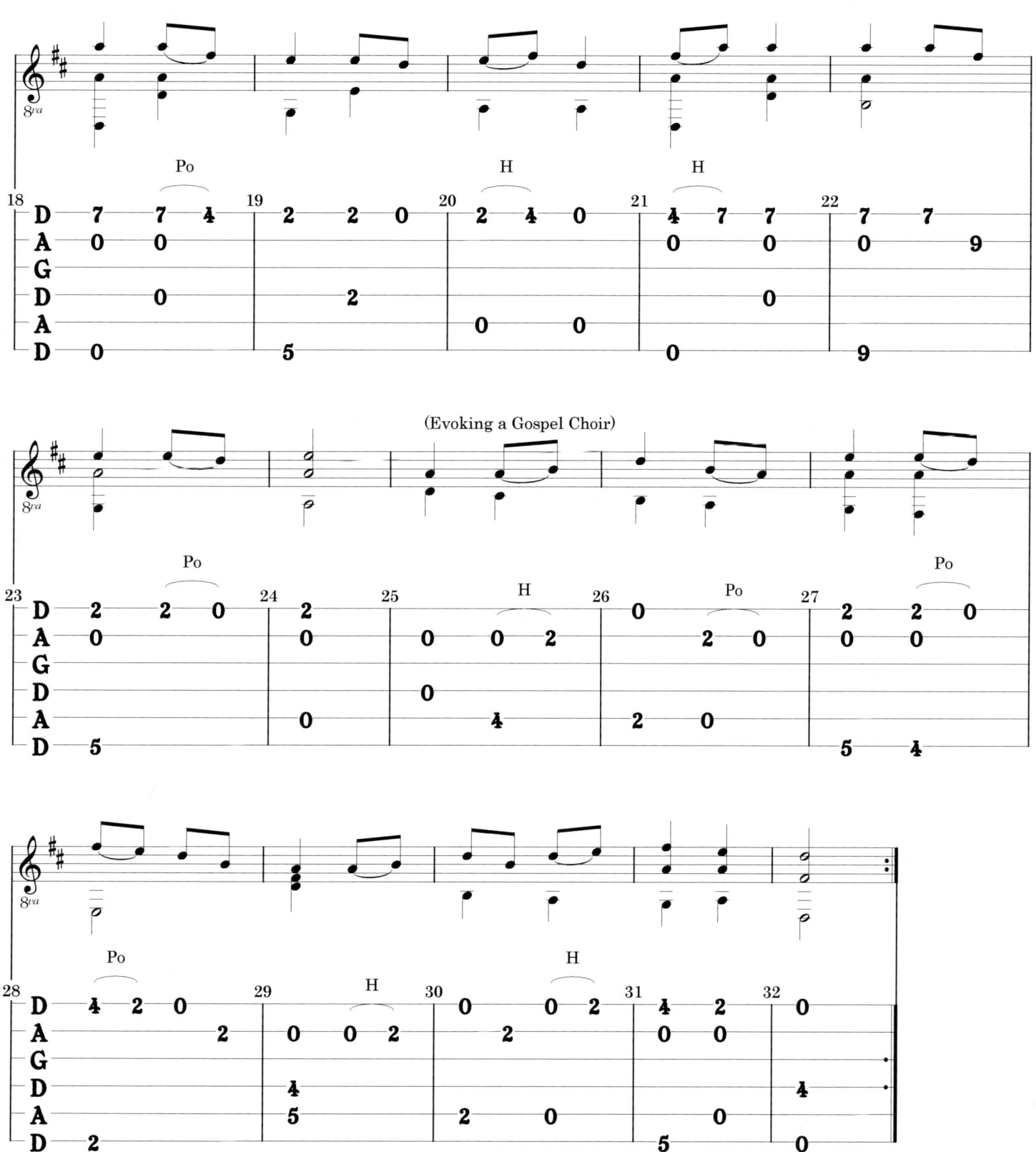

In Christ There is No East or West

Guitar Arr. (c) 2019 Ellsworth McMeen. All Rights Reserved. Used by Permission.

In Christ There is No East or West (Page 2/2)

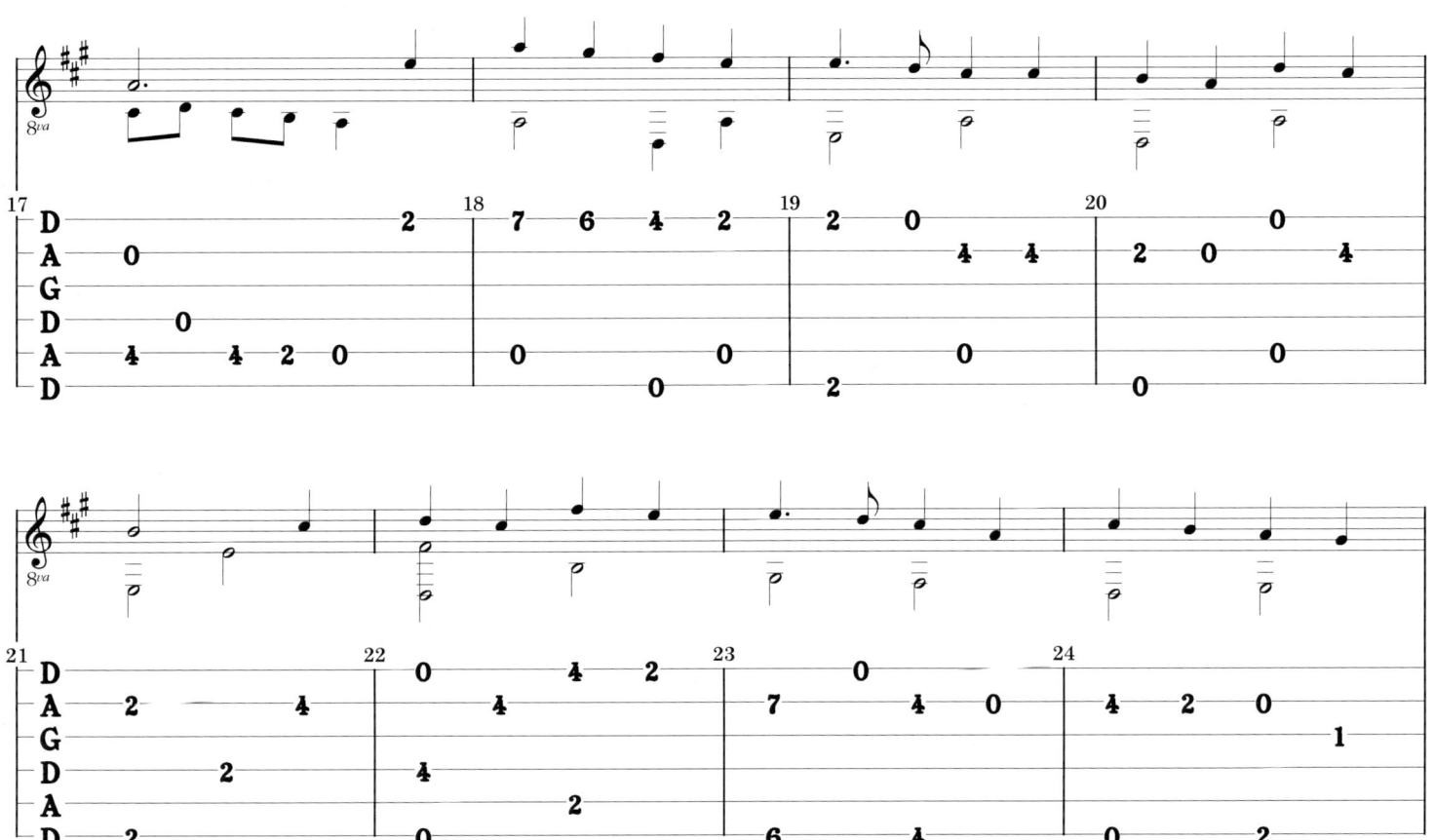

In the Great Triumphant Morning

Robert Emmett Winset
Arr. Ellsworth McMeen

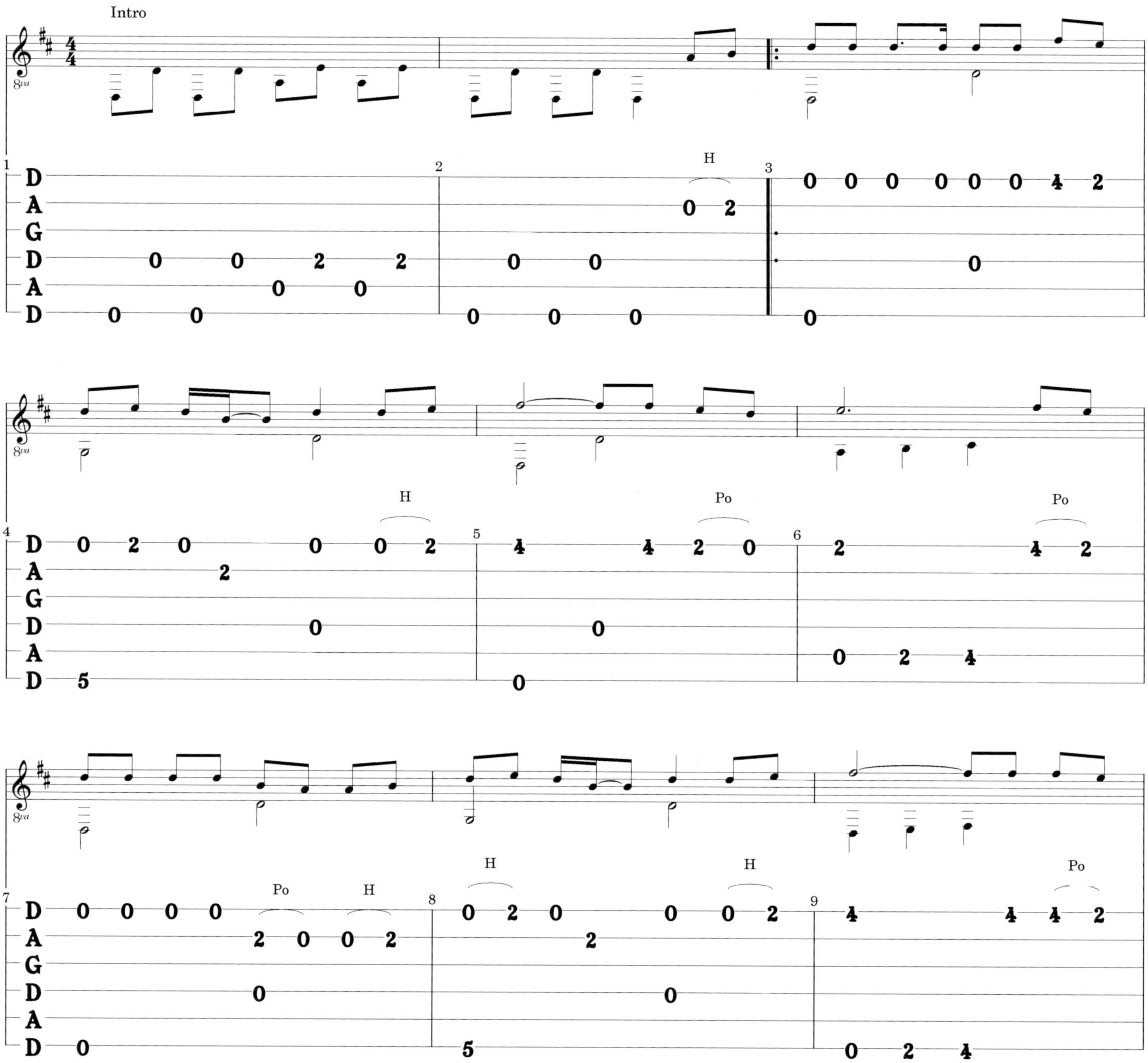

In the Great Triumphant Morning (Page 2/2)

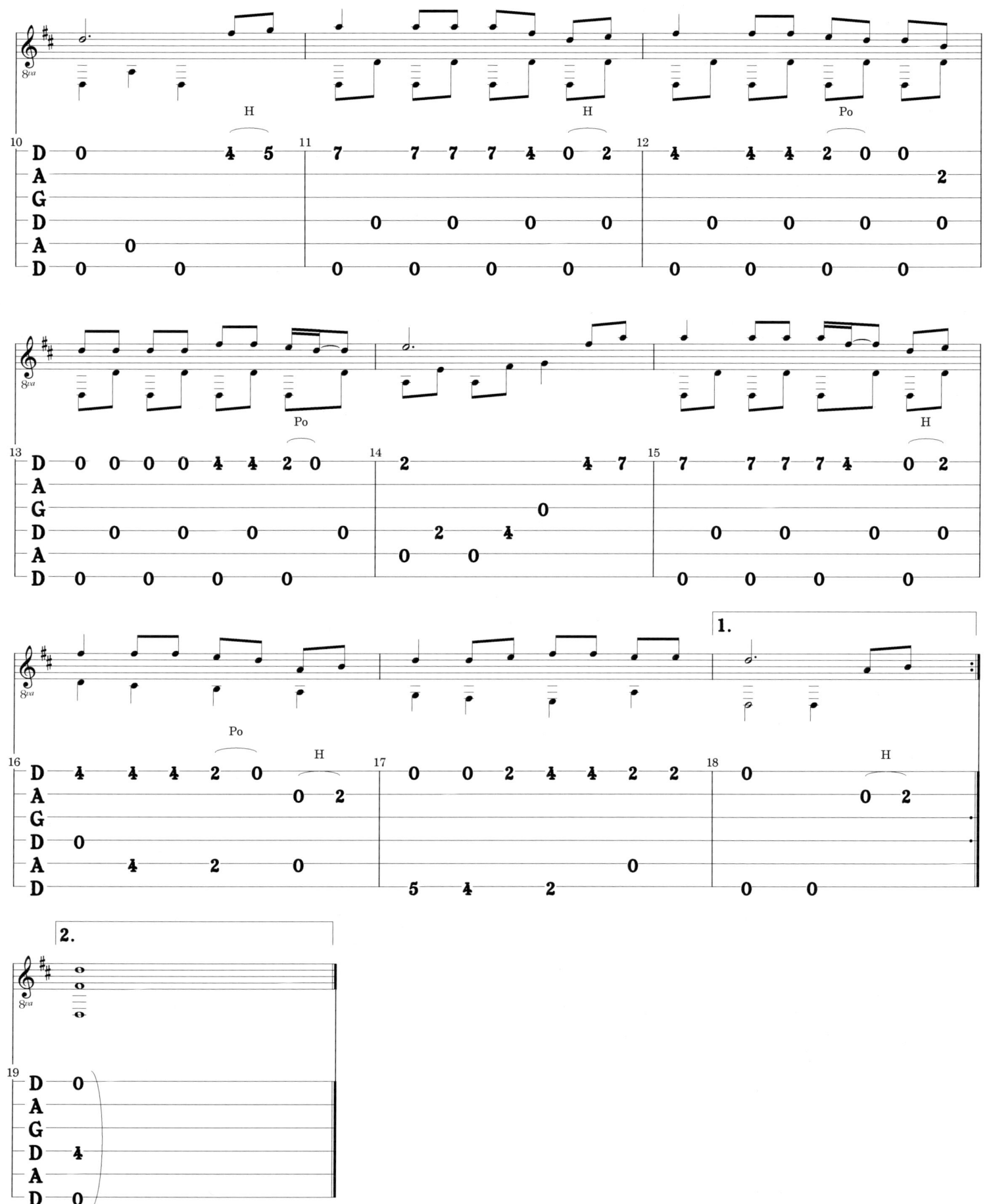

Just As I Am

William B. Bradbury; Charlotte Elliott
Arr. Ellsworth McMeen
(Thanks to Gene Zasadinski)

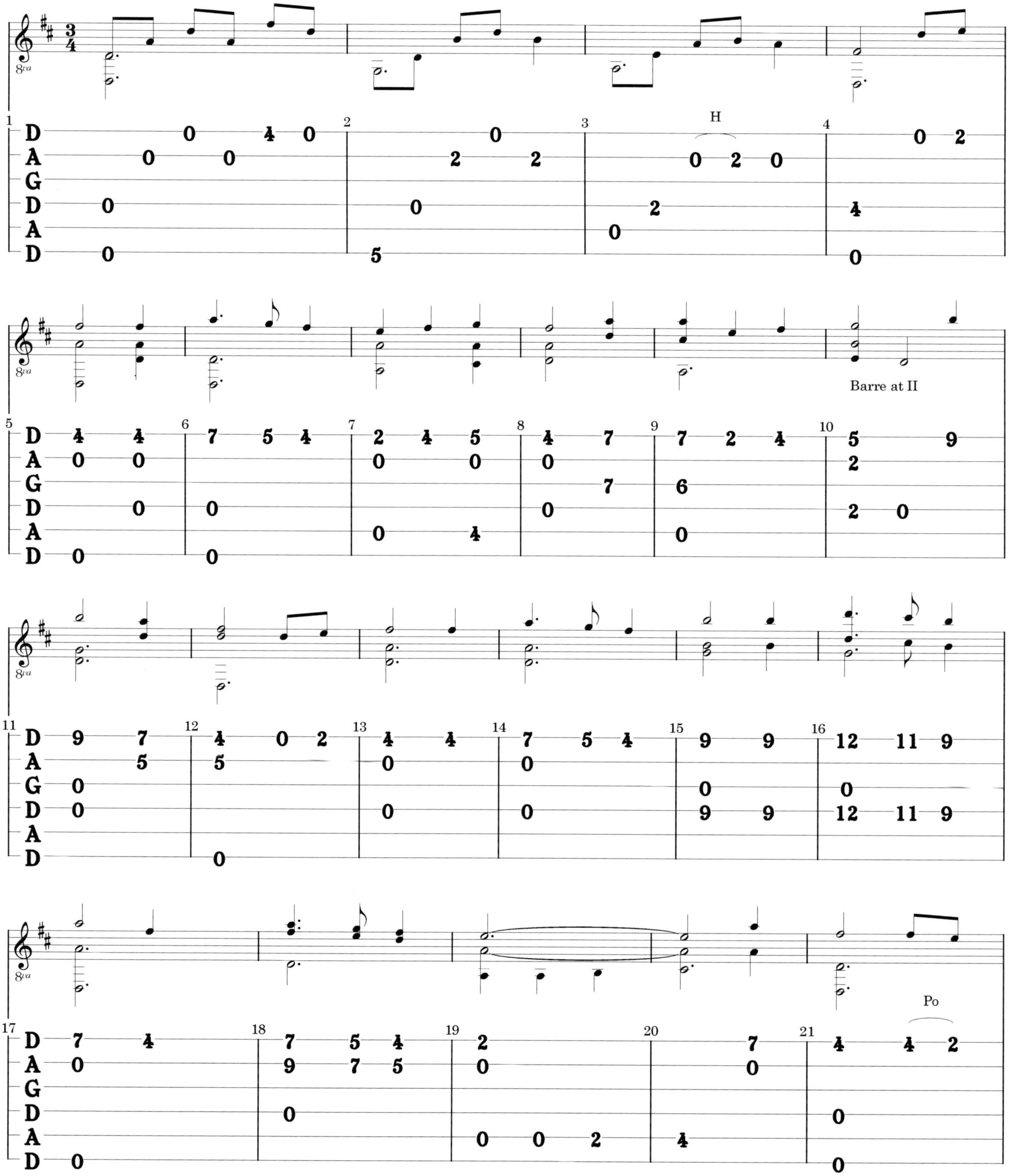

Guitar Arr. (c) 2019 Ellsworth McMeen. All Rights Reserved. Used by Permission.

Just As I Am (Page 2/2)

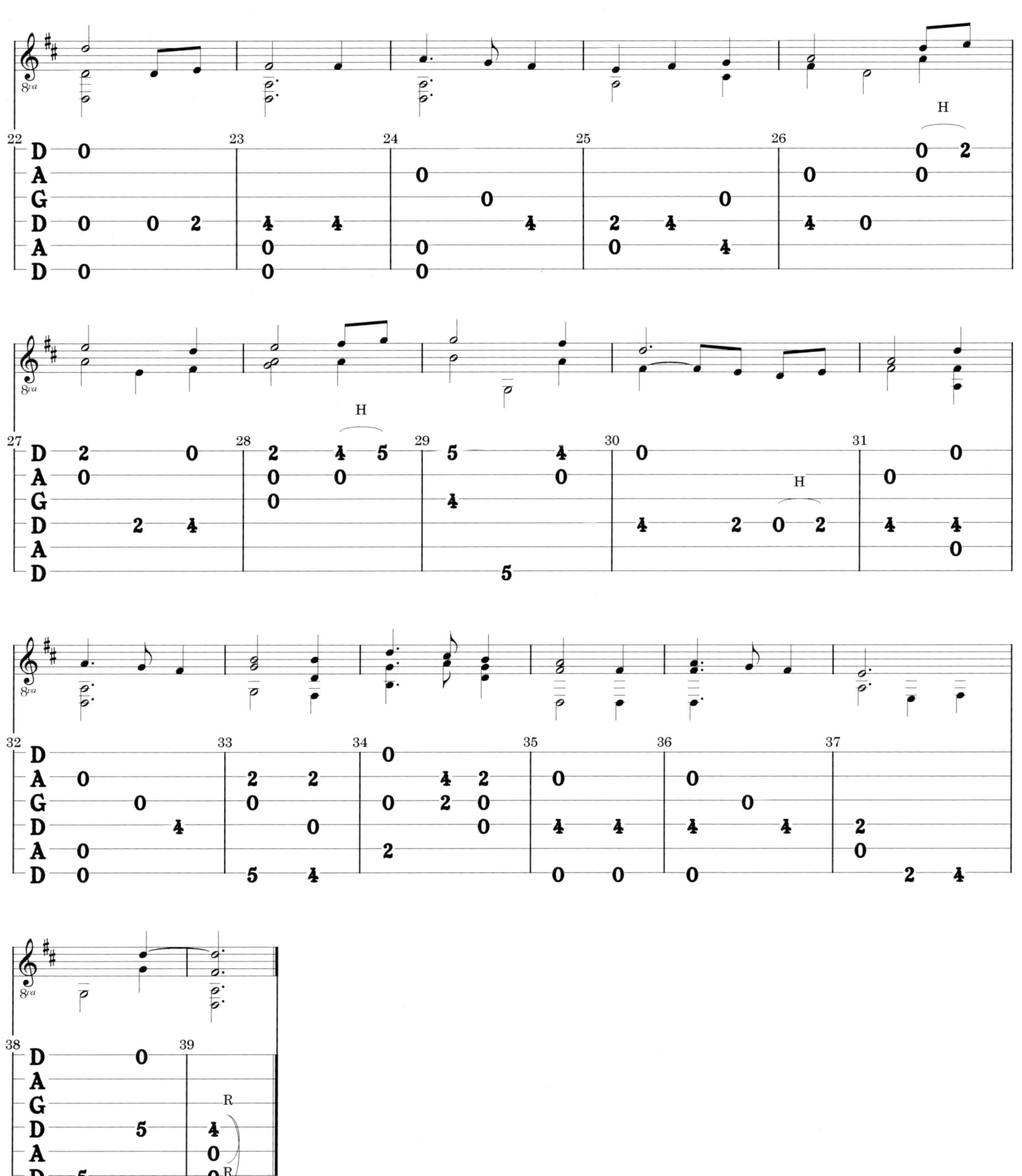

Must Jesus Bear the Cross Alone?

Guitar Arr. (c) 2019 Ellsworth McMeen. All Rights Reserved. Used by Permission.

Must Jesus Bear the Cross Alone? (Page 2/2)

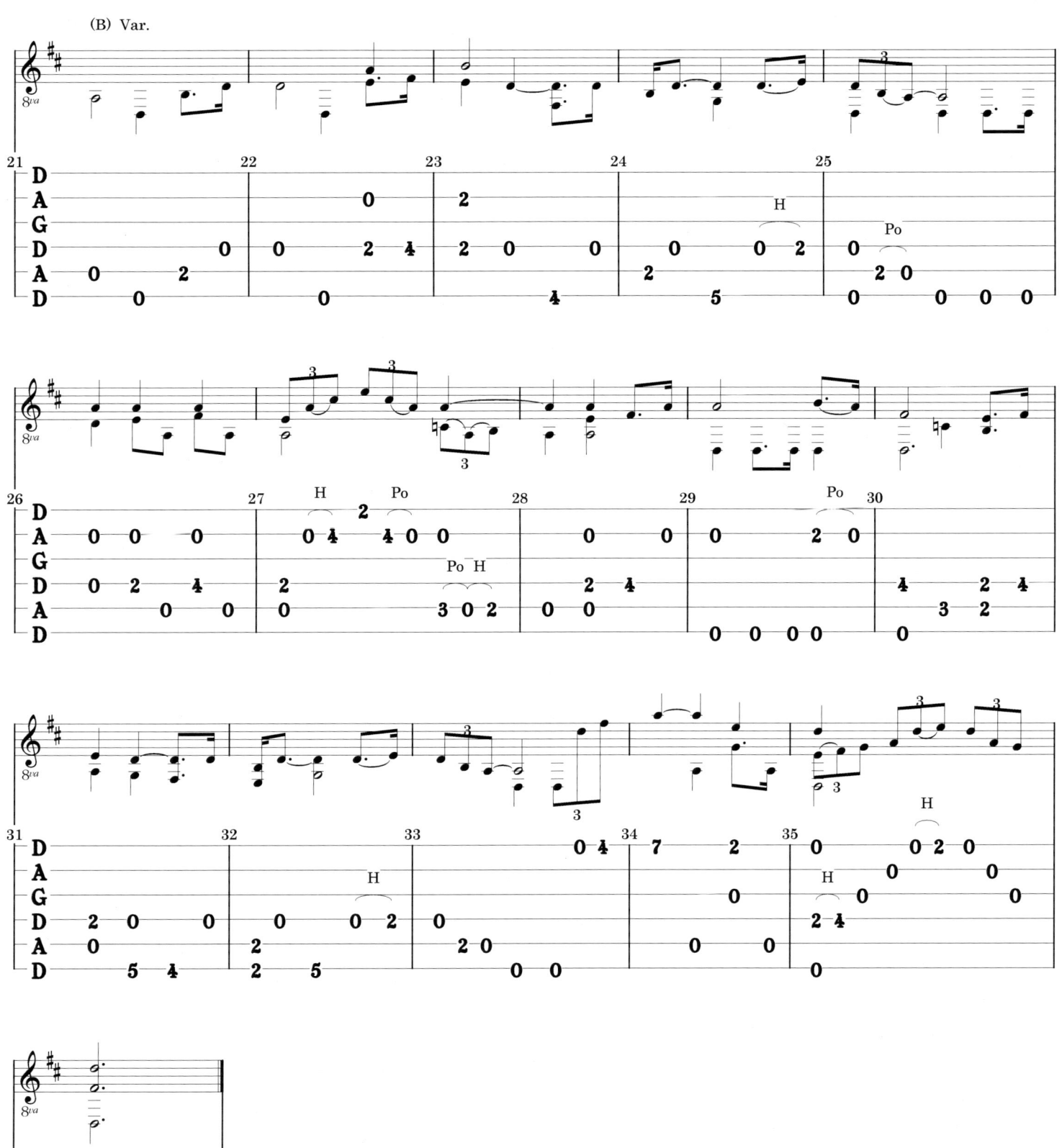

On Jordan's Stormy Banks

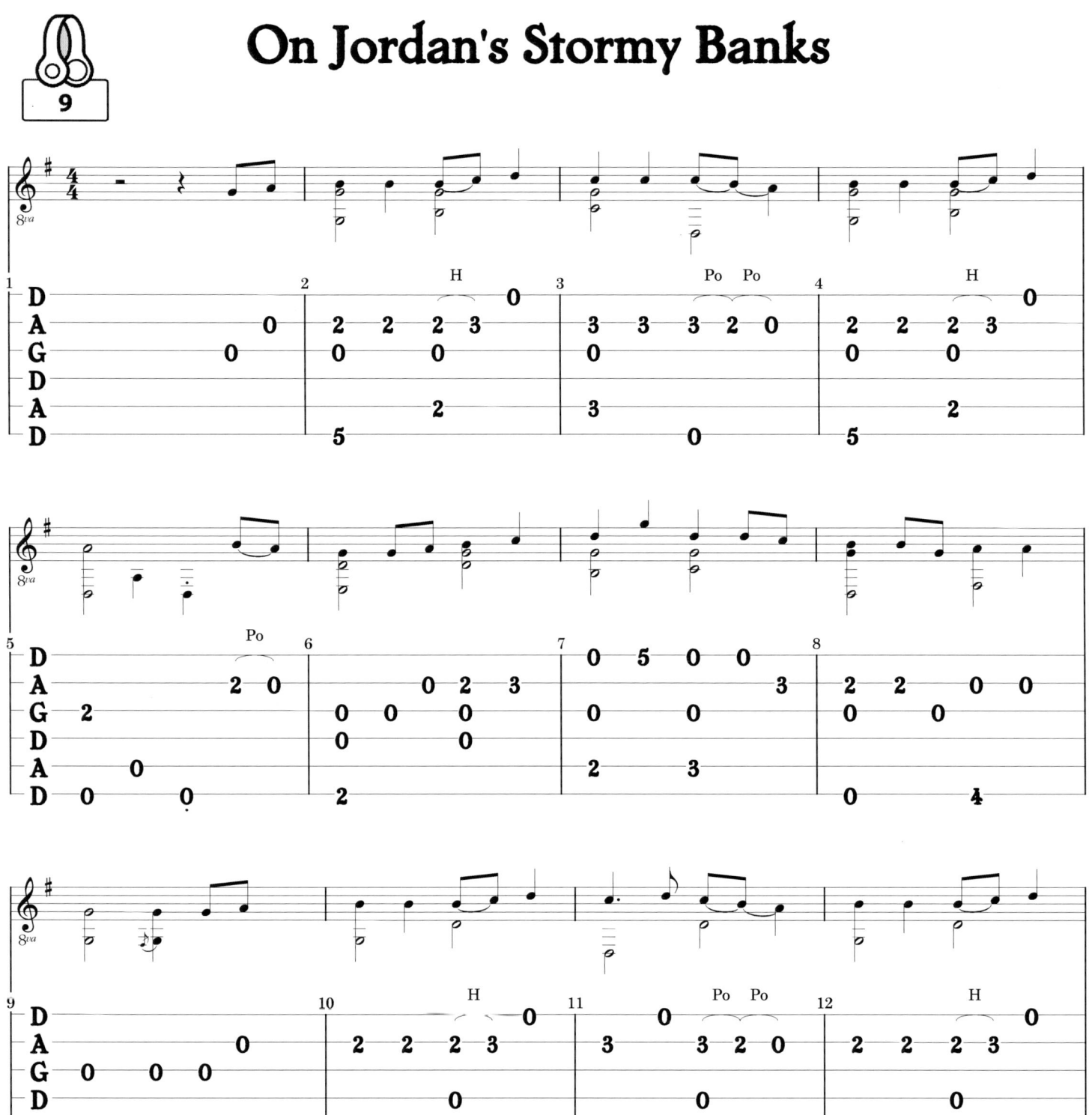

Guitar Arr. (c) 2019 Sandy Shalk. All Rights Reserved. Used by Permission.

On Jordan's Stormy Banks (Page 2/3)

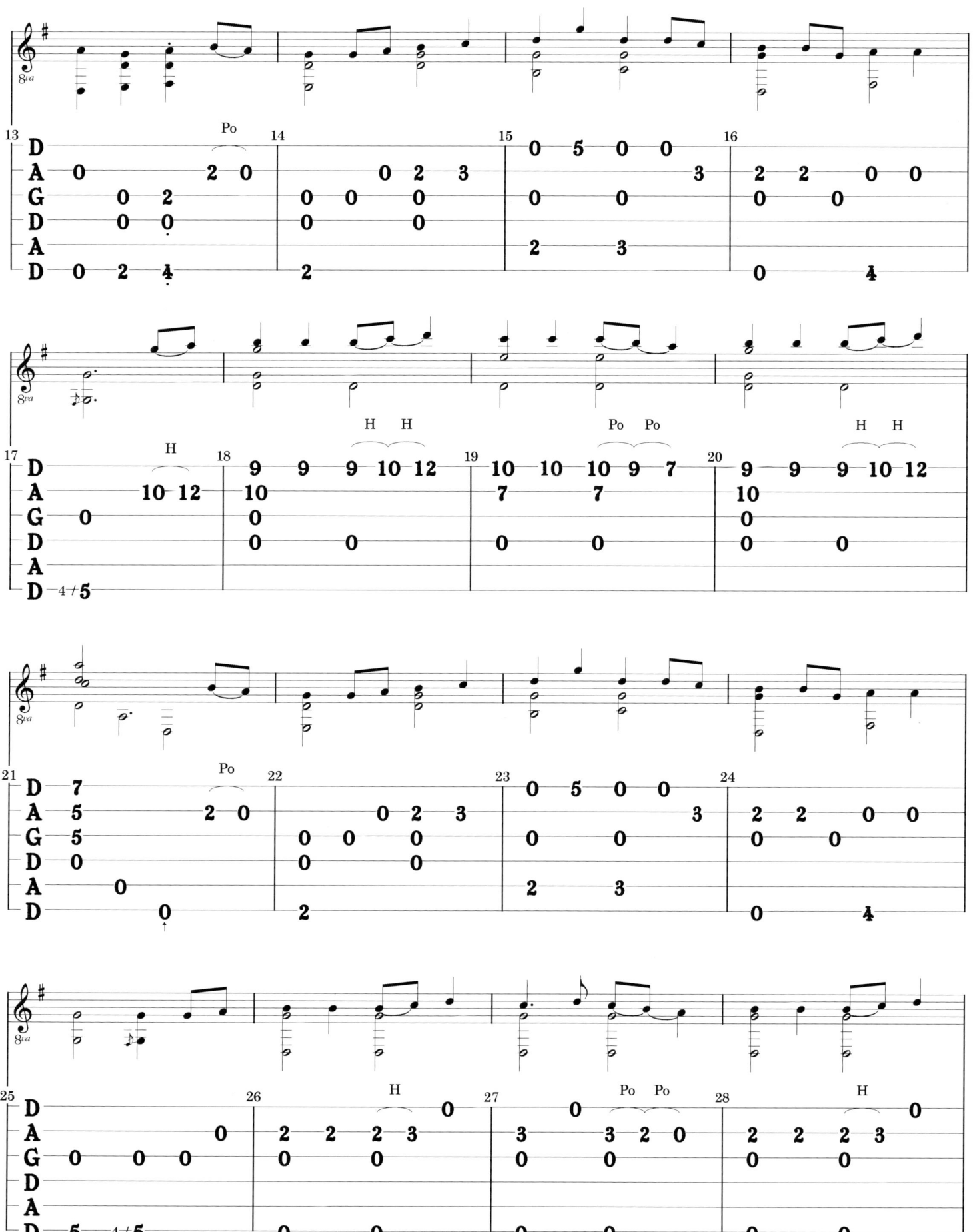

On Jordan's Stormy Banks (Page 3/3)

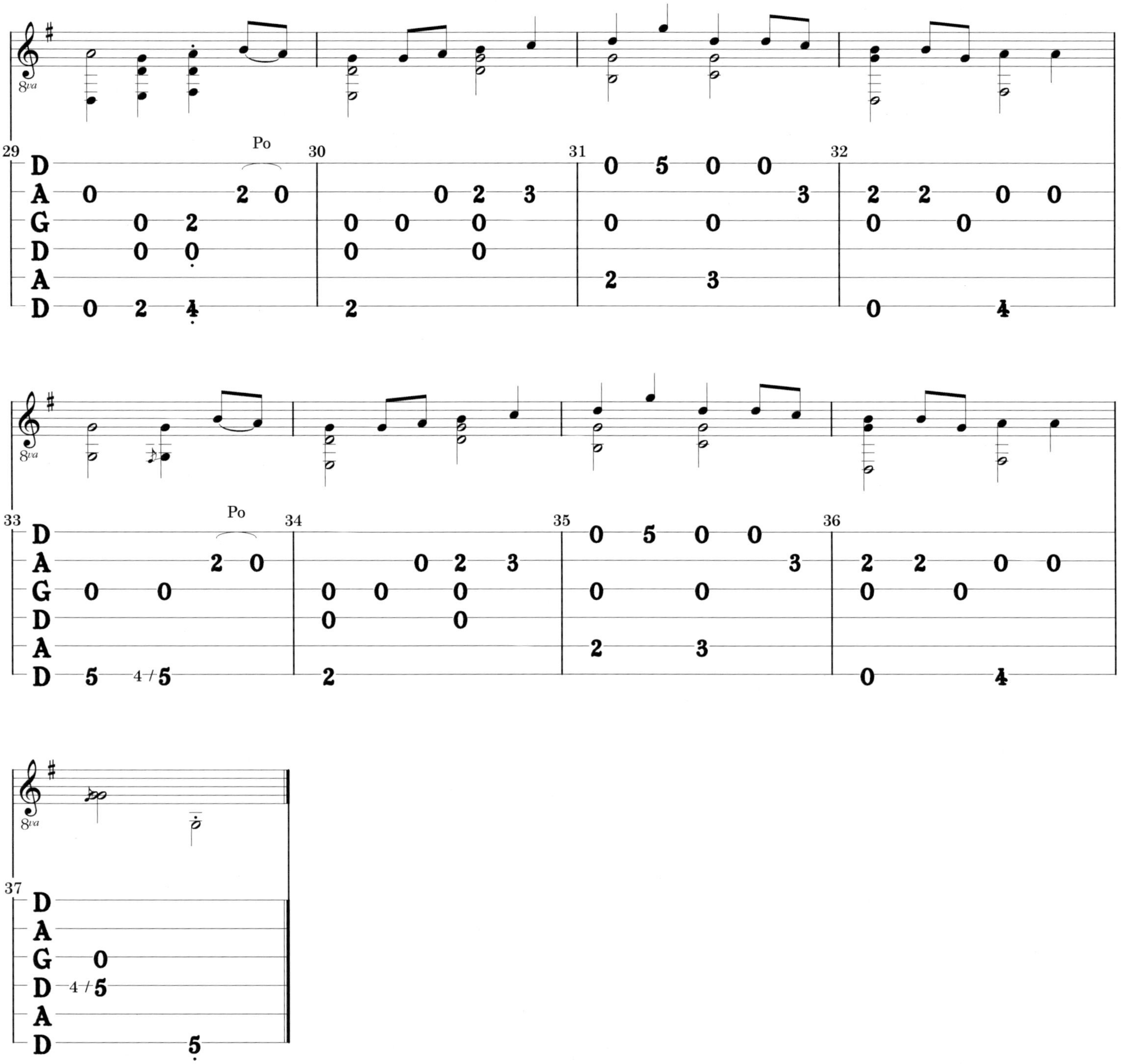

This page has been left blank to avoid an awkward page turn.

Softly and Tenderly

Will L. Thompson
Arr. Sandy Shalk

Guitar Arr. (c) 2019 Sandy Shalk. All Rights Reserved. Used by Permission.

Softly and Tenderly (Page 2/3)

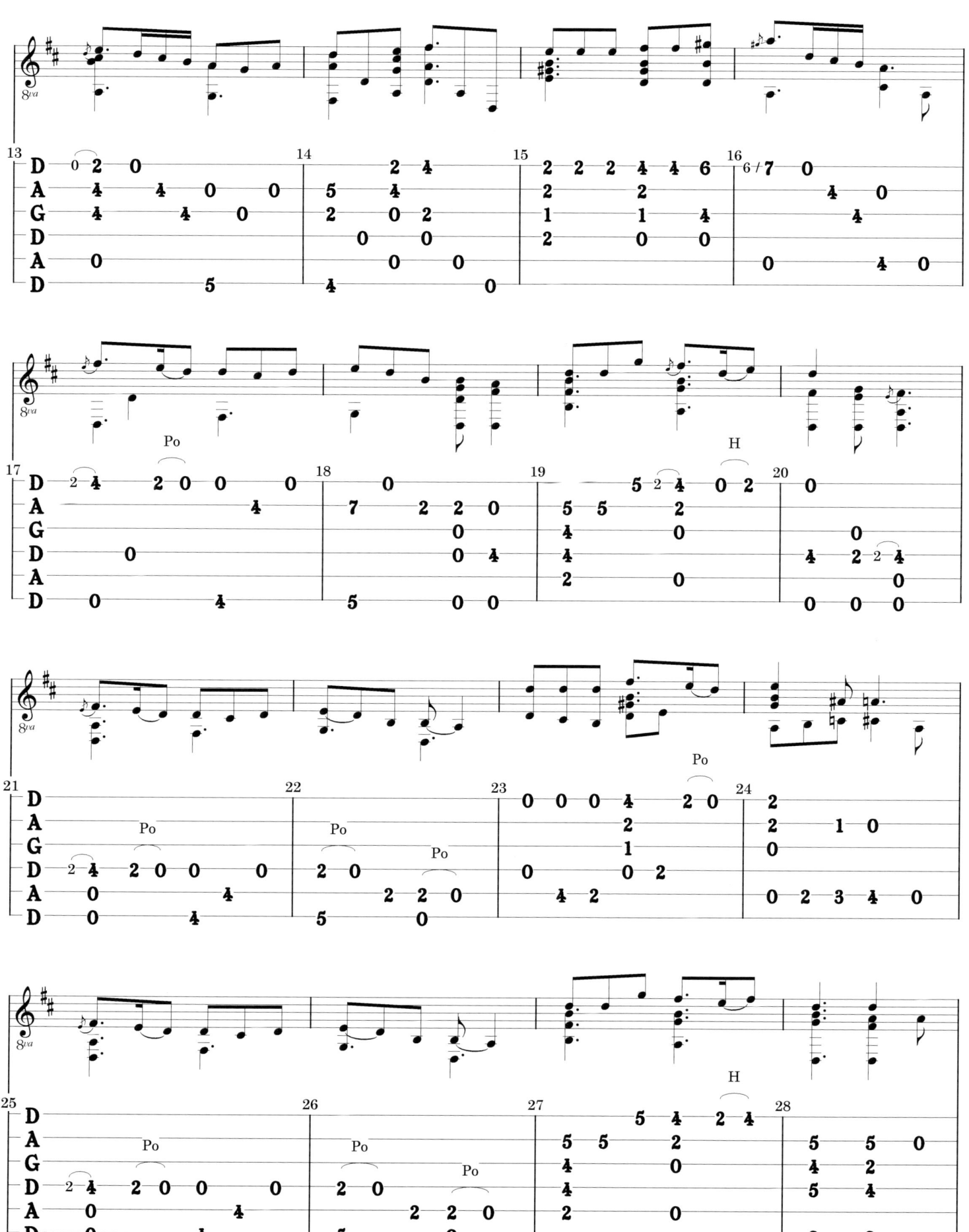

Softly and Tenderly (Page 3/3)

This page has been left blank to avoid an awkward page turn.

The Hallelujah Side

Johnson Oatman, Jr.
Arr. Ellsworth McMeen

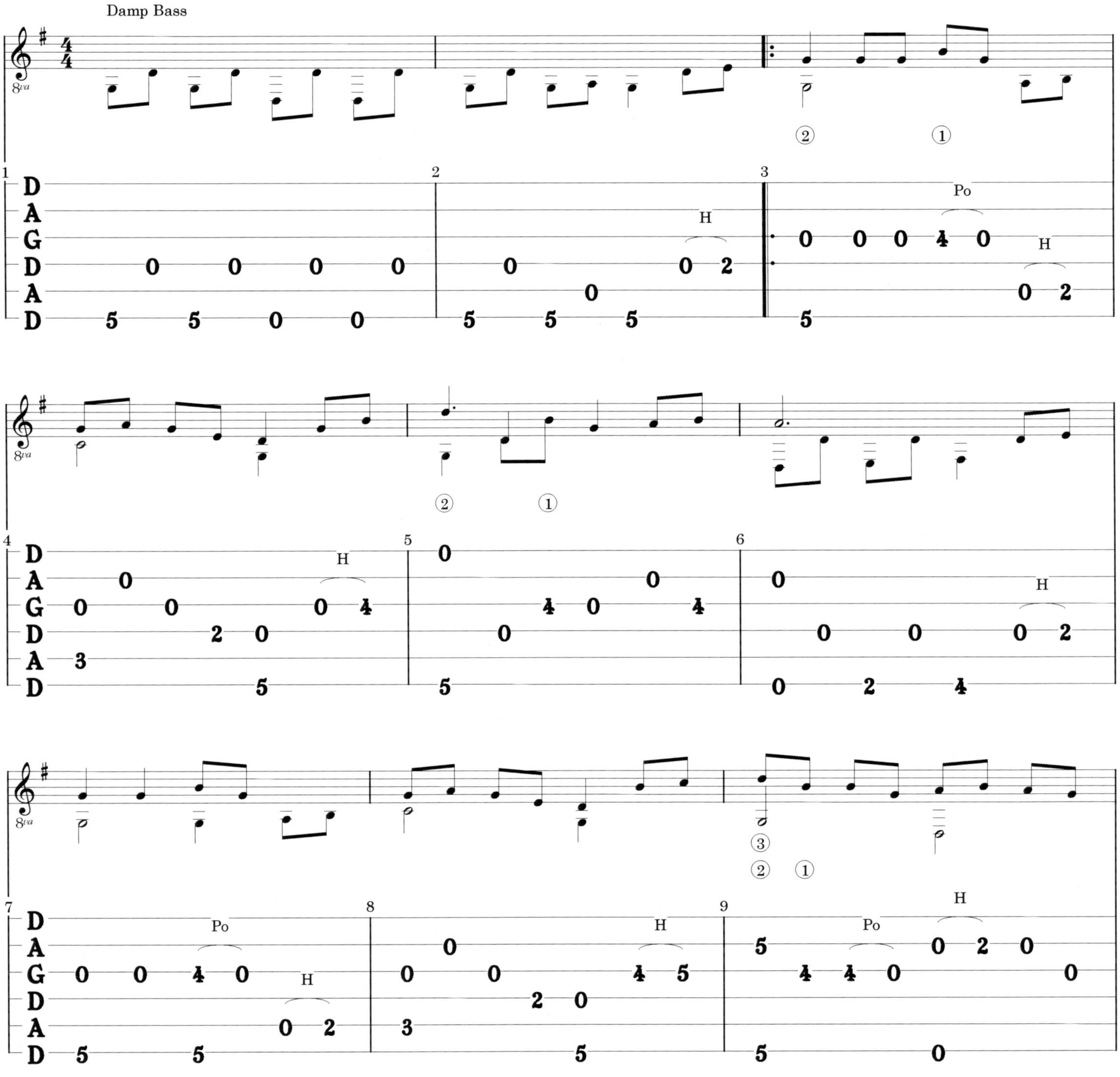

The Hallelujah Side (Page 2/2)

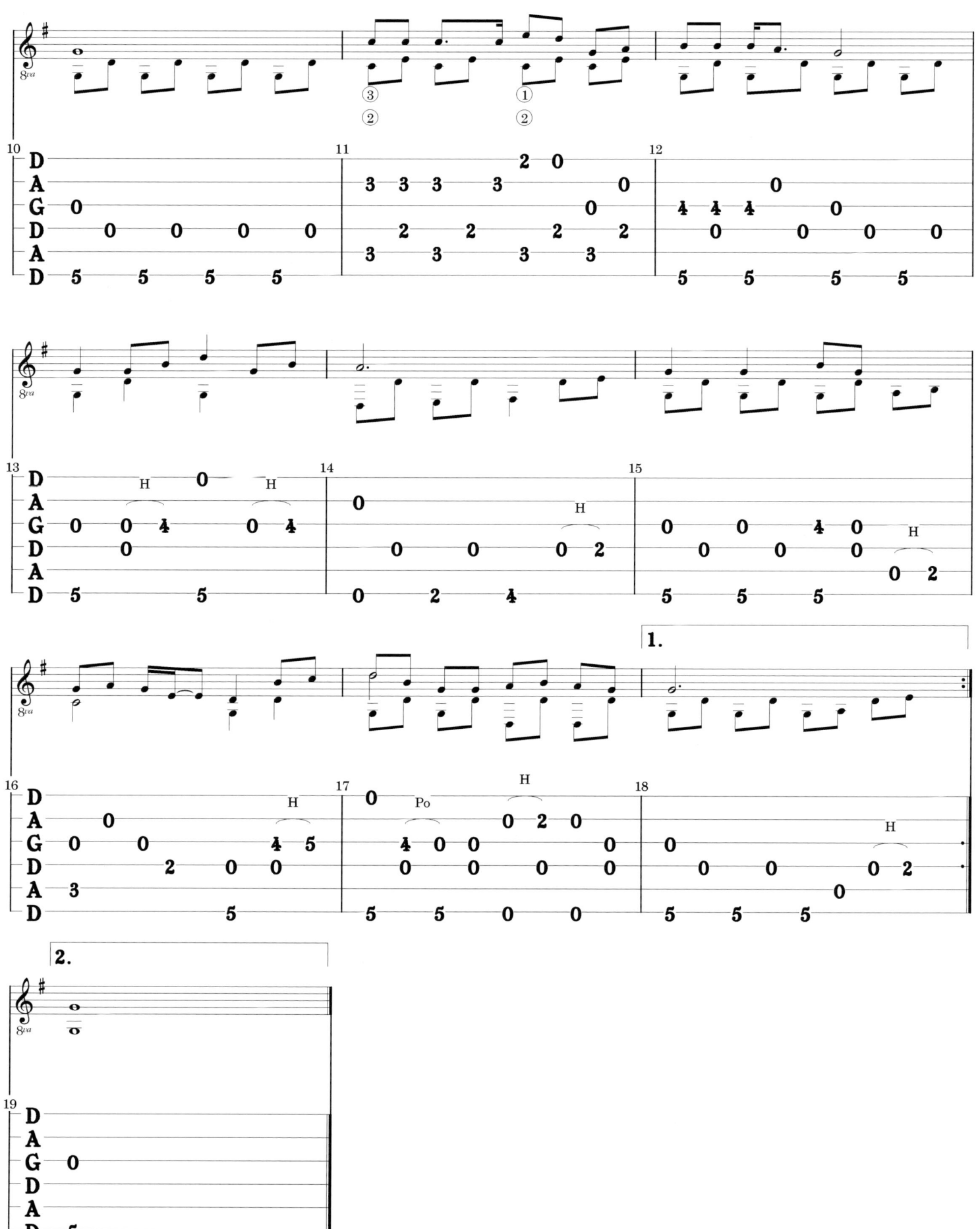

There Is Power in the Blood

Lewis E. Jones
Arr. Ellsworth McMeen

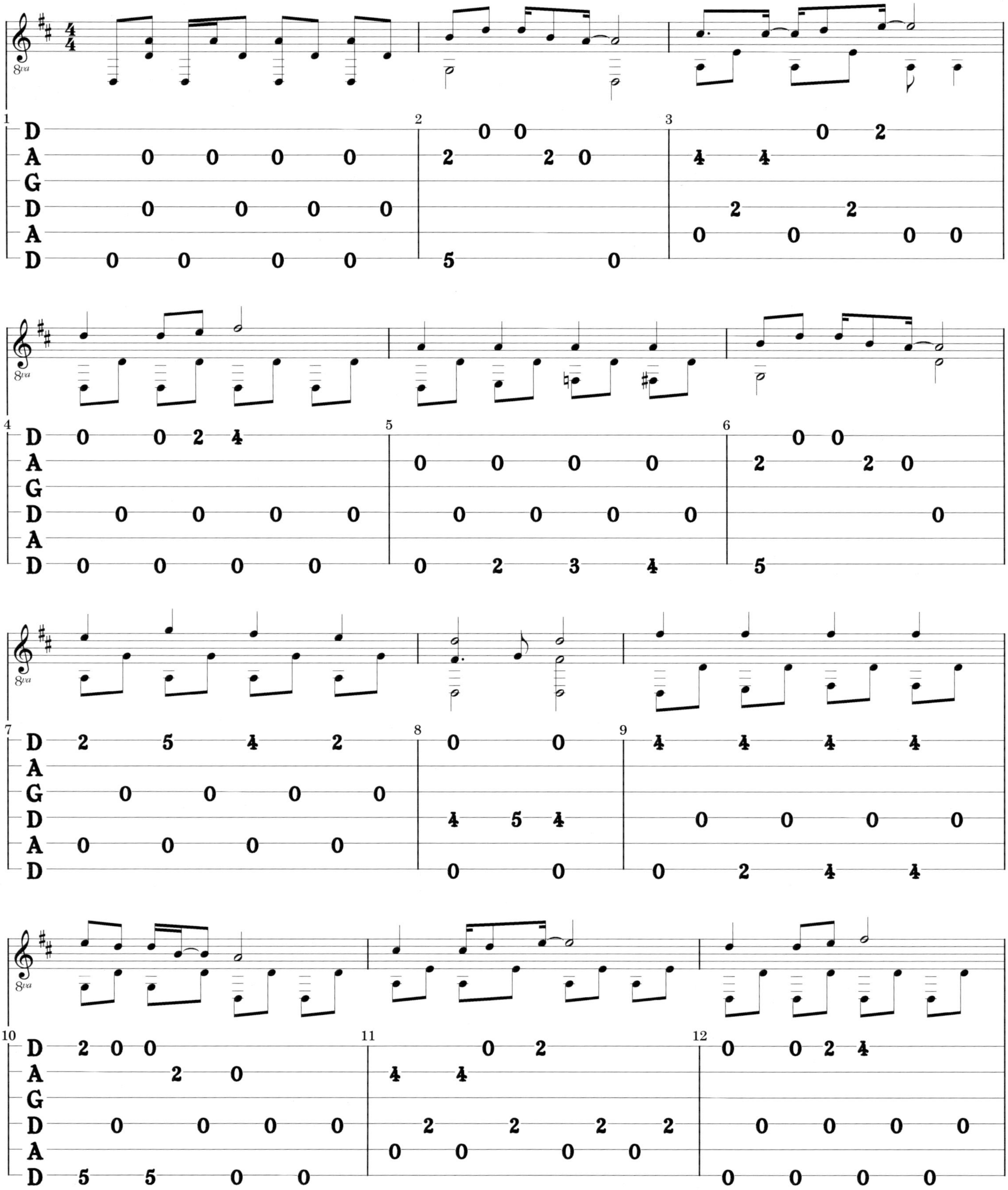

Guitar Arr. (c) 2019 Ellsworth McMeen. All Rights Reserved. Used by Permission.

There Is Power in the Blood (Page 2/2)

What a Friend We Have in Jesus

Charles C. Converse
Arr. Ellsworth McMeen

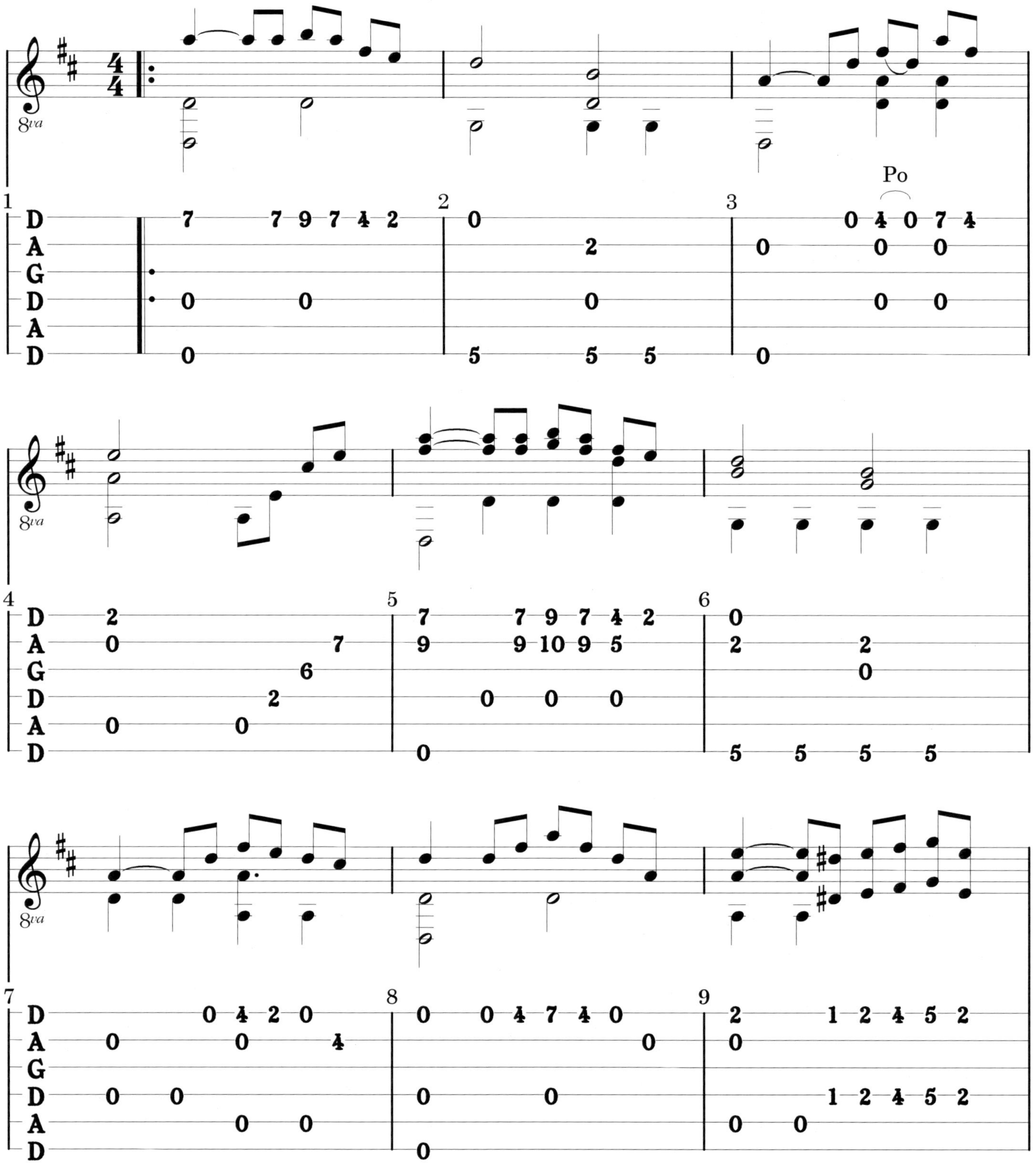

What a Friend We Have in Jesus (Page 2/2)

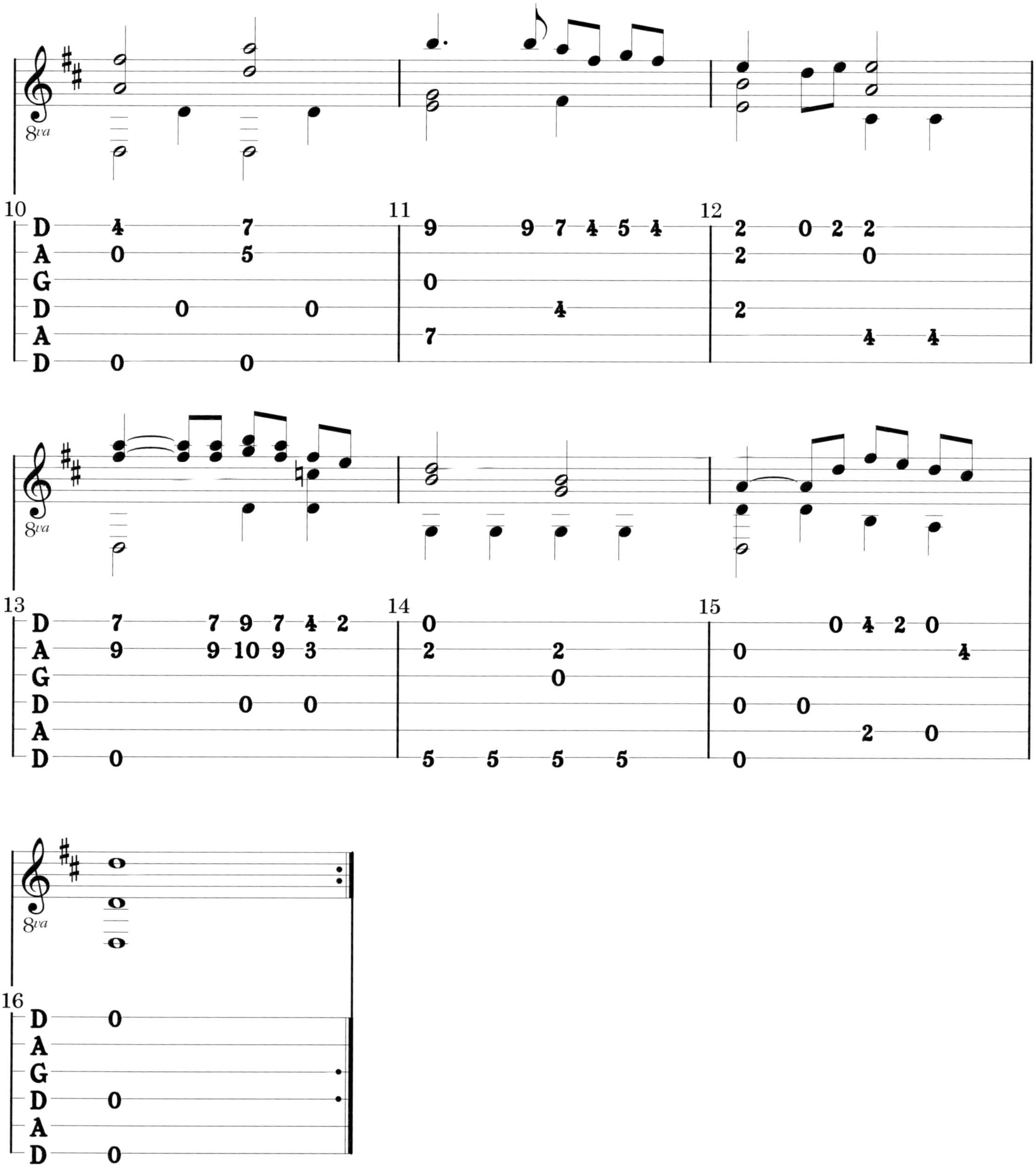

When I Can Read My Title Clear

J. C. Lowry; Isaac Watts
Arr. Sandy Shalk

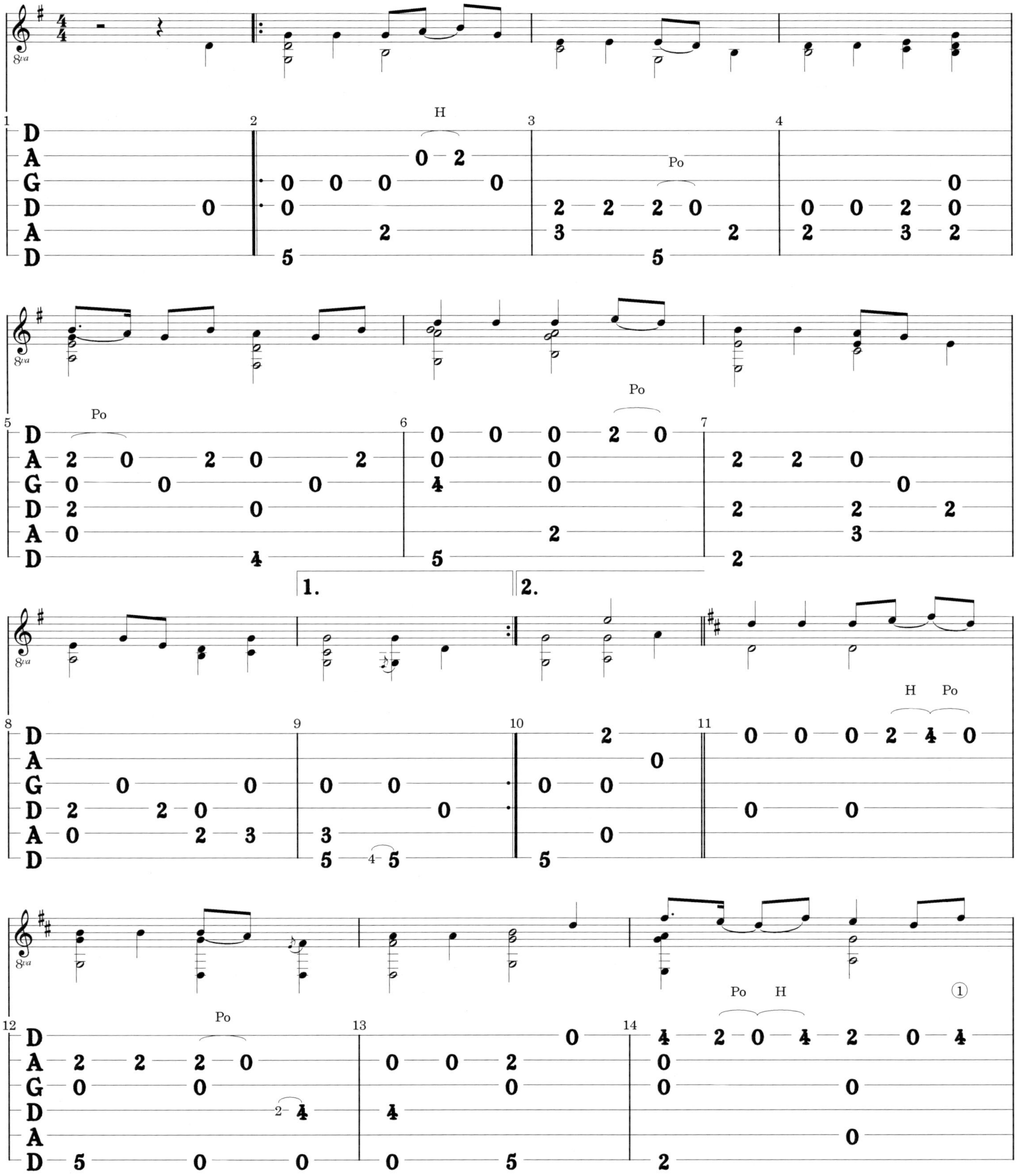

When I Can Read My Title Clear (Page 2/2)

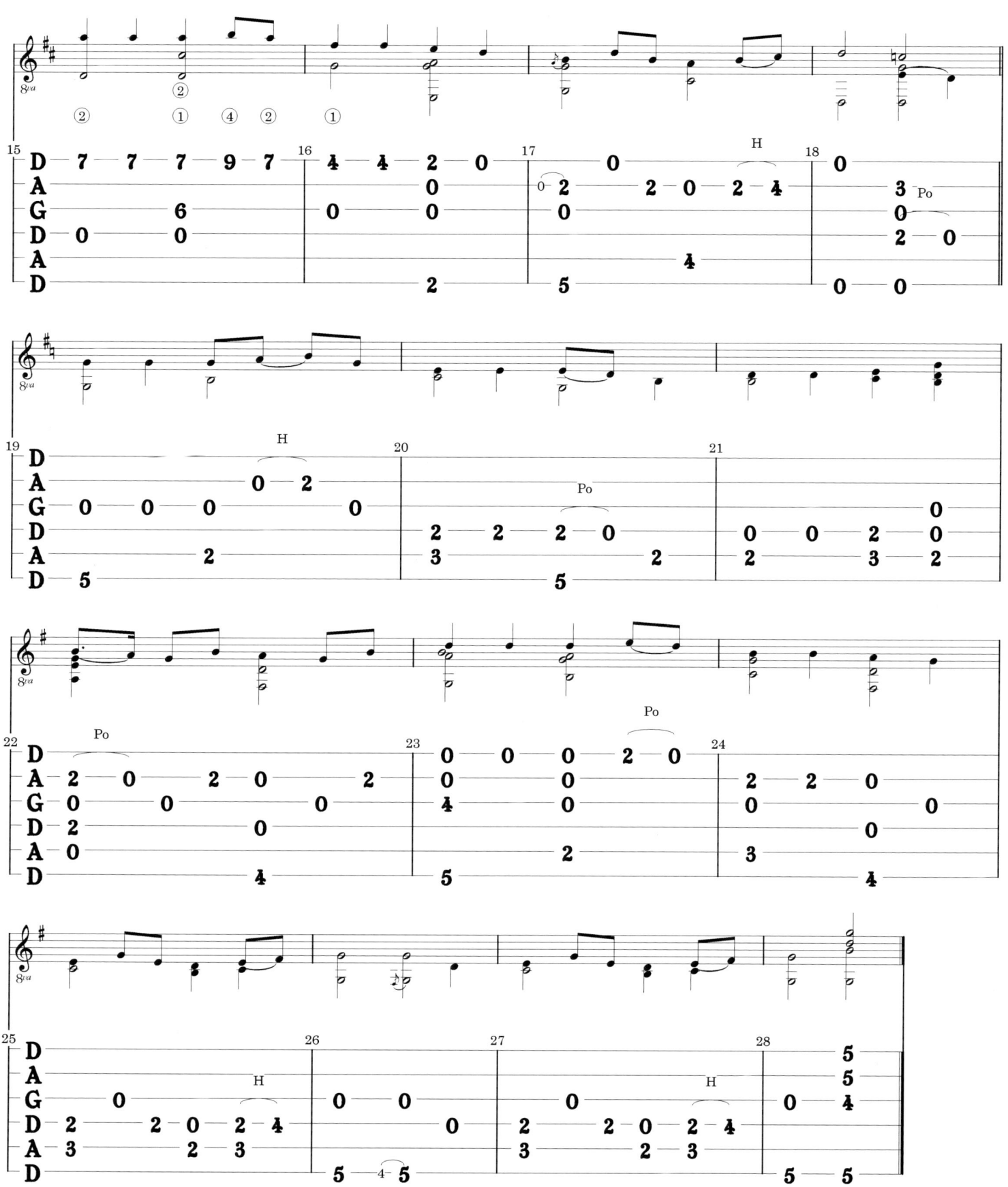

Whiter Than Snow

William G. Fischer
Arr. Sandy Shalk

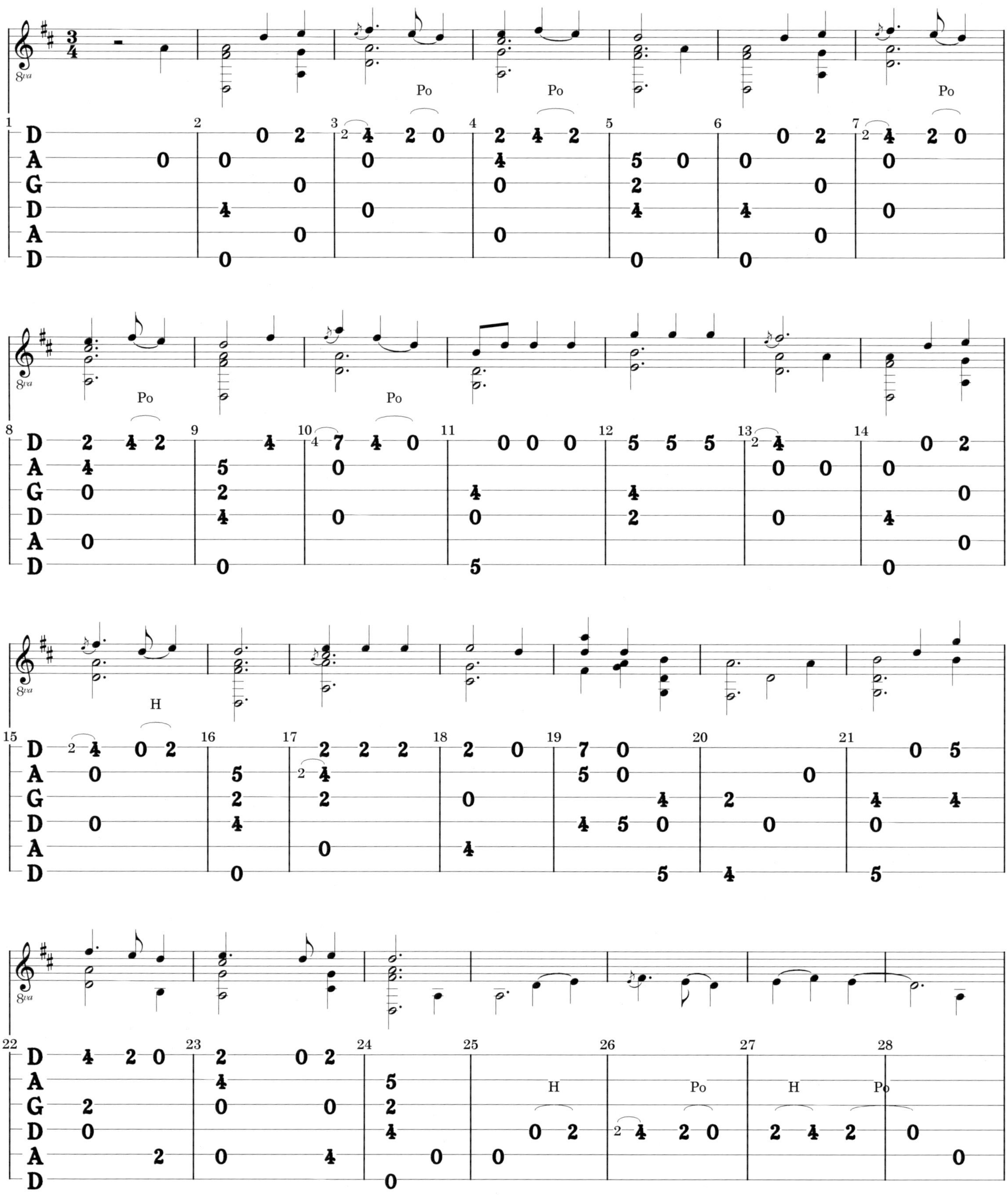

Whiter Than Snow (Page 2/2)

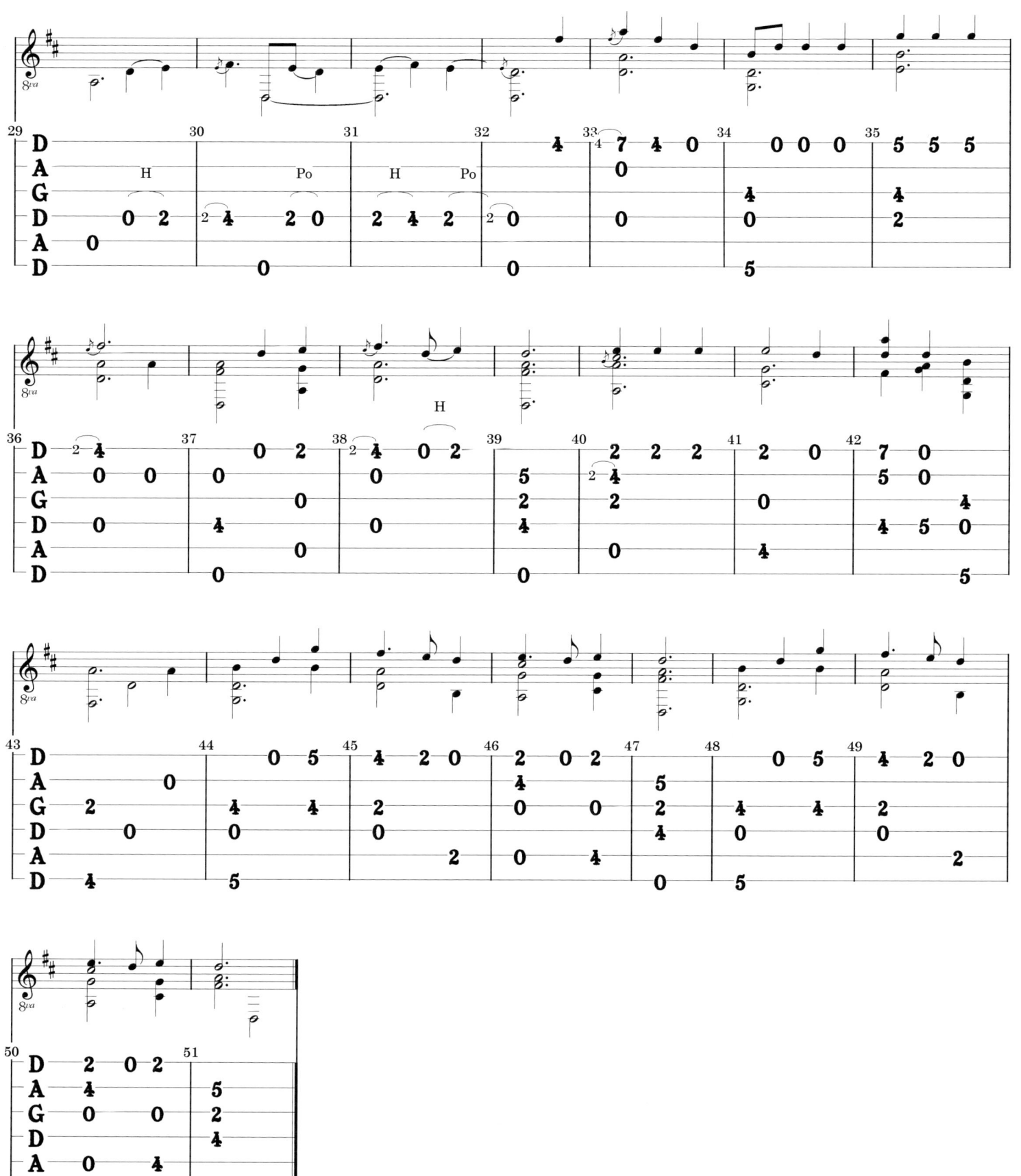

Will the Circle Be Unbroken

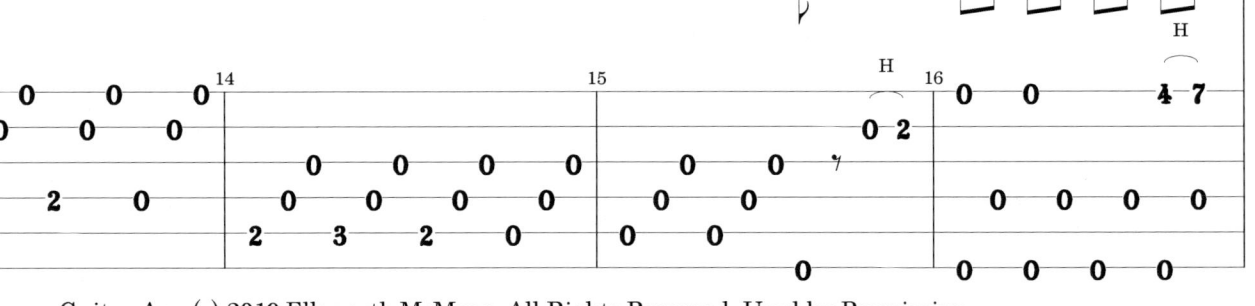

Will the Circle Be Unbroken (Page 2/2)

Yes, I Know

Anna W. Waterman
Arr. Sandy Shalk

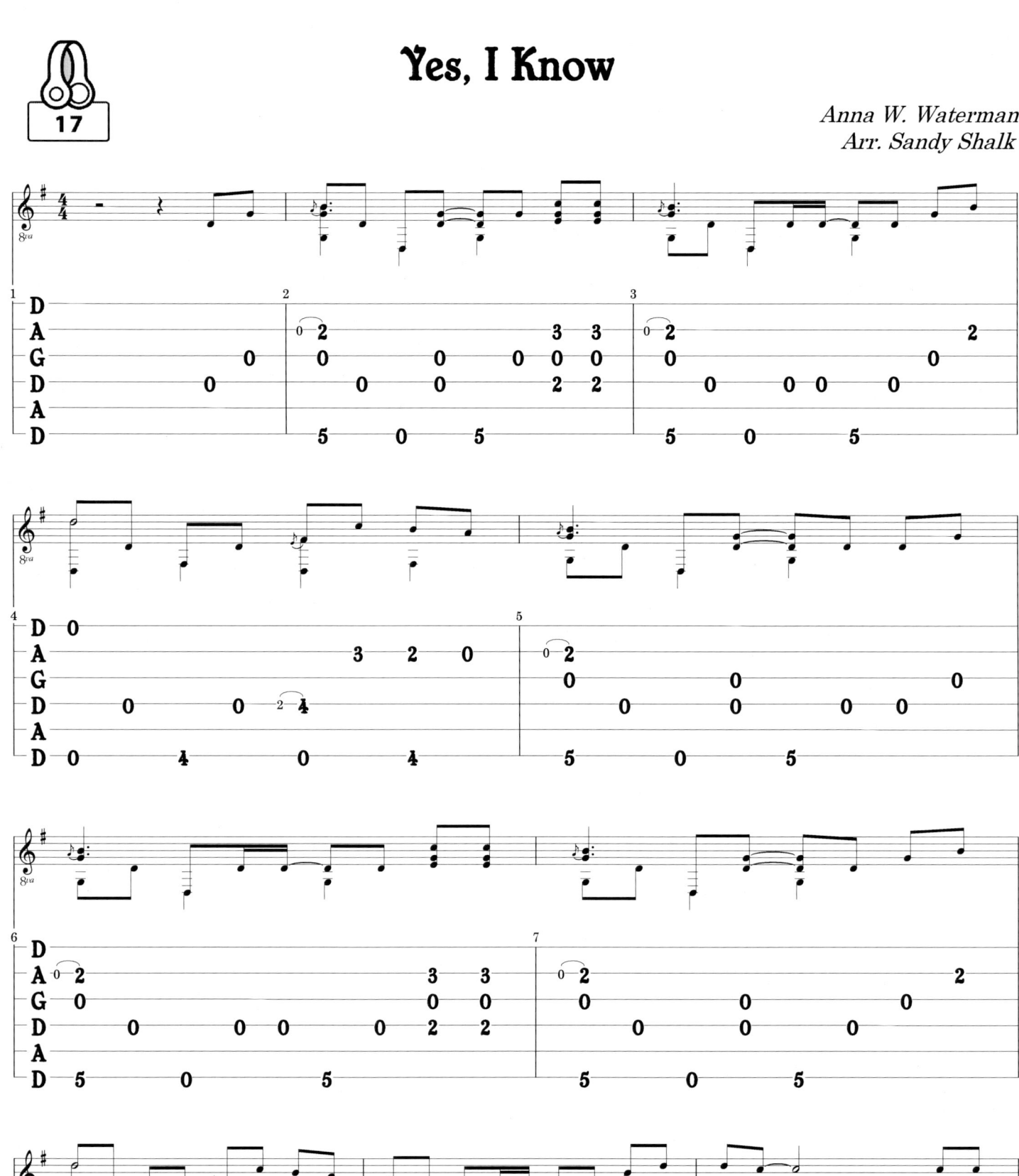

Yes, I Know (Page 2/3)

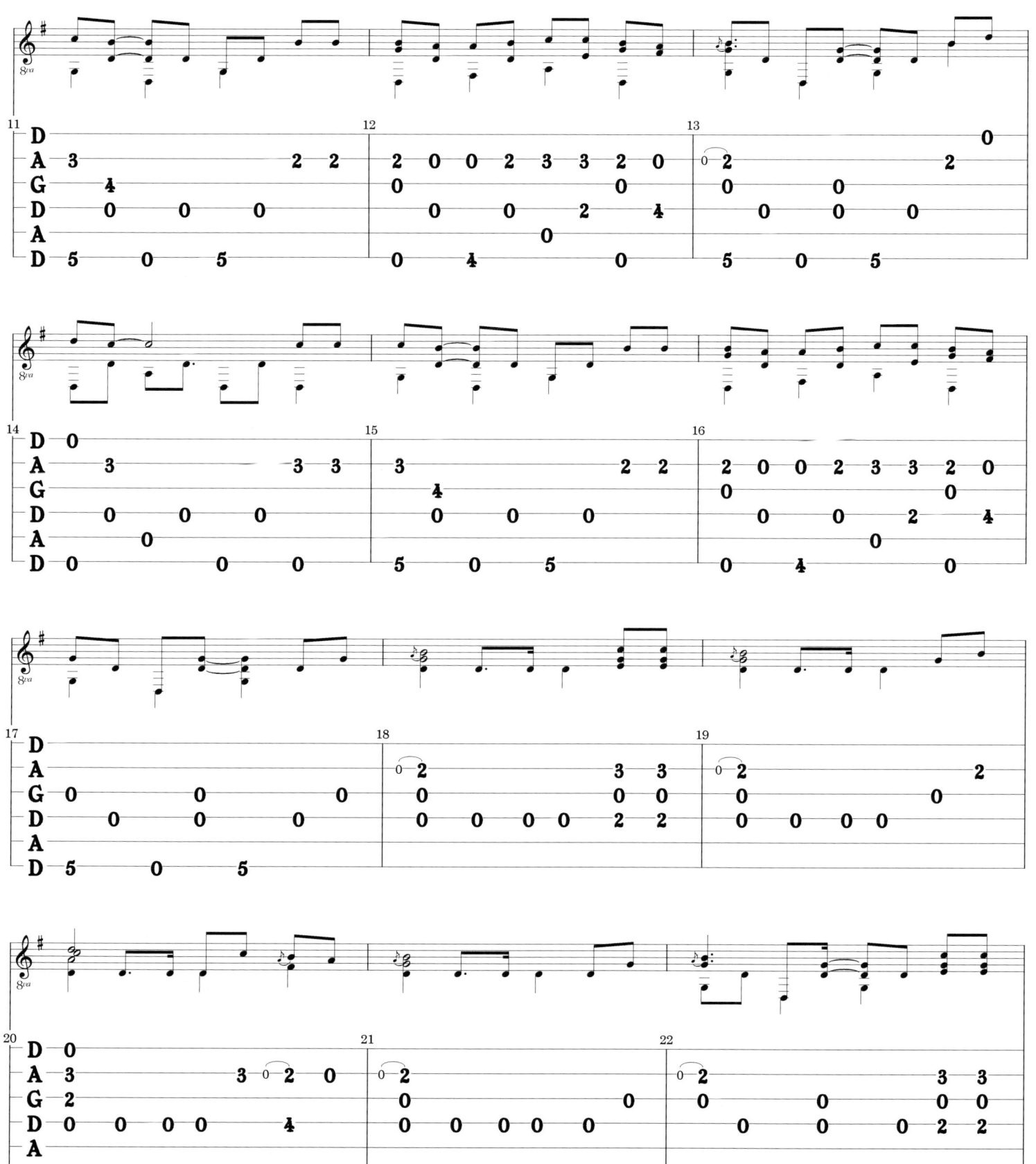

Yes, I Know (Page 3/3)

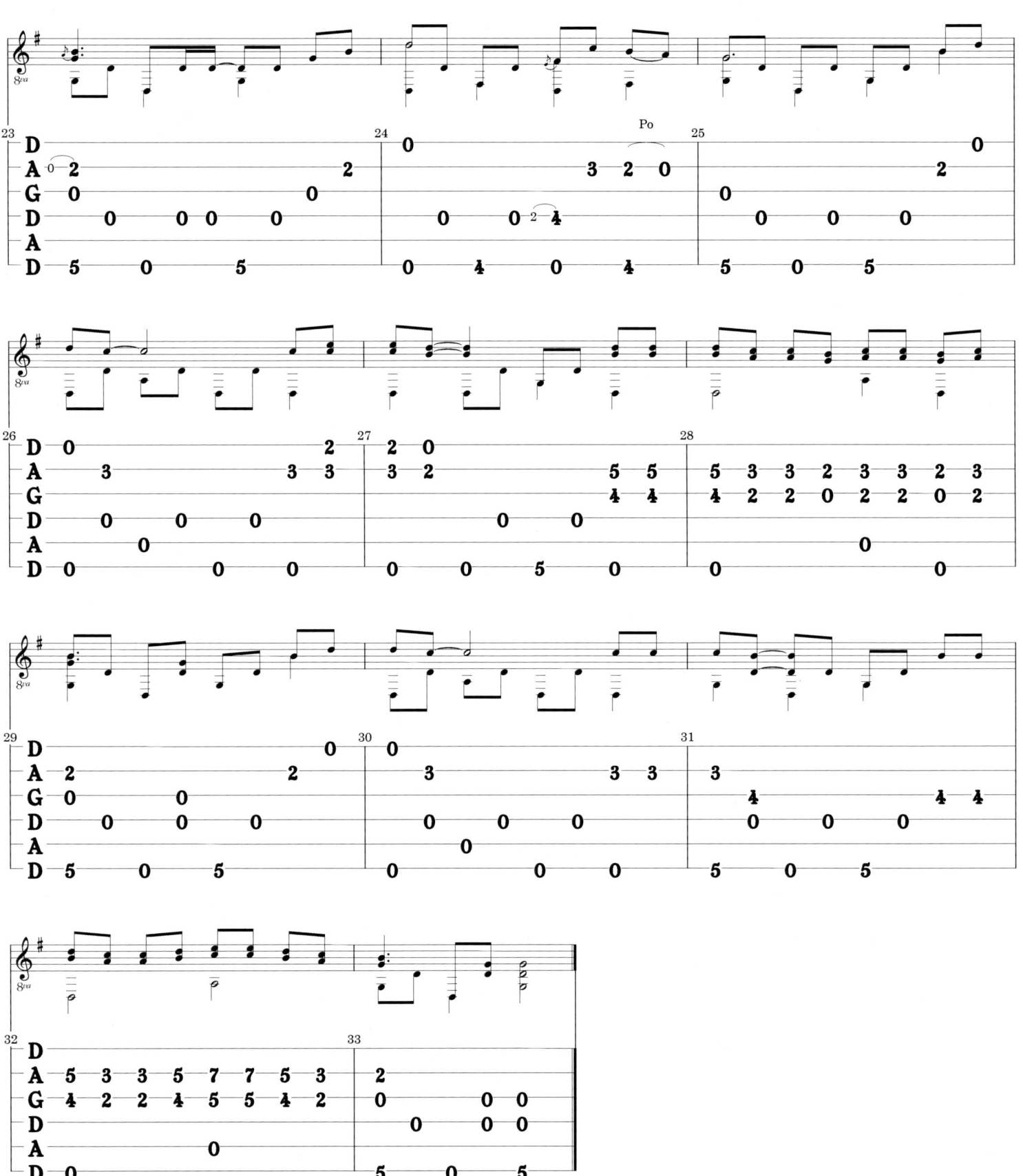

El McMeen   Sandy Shalk

Psalm 150

(King James Version)

¹Praise ye the LORD. Praise God in his sanctuary: praise him in the firmament of his power.

² Praise him for his mighty acts: praise him according to his excellent greatness.

³ Praise him with the sound of the trumpet: praise him with the psaltery and harp.

⁴ Praise him with the timbrel and dance: praise him with stringed instruments and organs.

⁵ Praise him upon the loud cymbals: praise him upon the high sounding cymbals.

⁶ Let every thing that hath breath praise the LORD. Praise ye the LORD.